THE DIALECTIC OF ACADEMIC LIBRARIANSHIP:

A CRITICAL APPROACH

THE DIALECTIC OF ACADEMIC LIBRARIANSHIP:

A CRITICAL APPROACH

Stephen Bales

LIBRARY JUICE PRESS
SACRAMENTO, CA

Copyright 2015 Stephen Bales

Published in 2015 by Library Juice Press

Library Juice Press
PO Box 188784
Sacramento, CA 95822

http://libraryjuicepress.com/

This book is printed on acid-free, sustainably-sourced paper.

Library of Congress Cataloging-in-Publication Data

Bales, Stephen.
The dialectic of academic libararianship: a critical approach / Stephen Bales.
   pages cm.
Includes bibliographical references and index.
   ISBN 978-1-936117-89-5 (alk. paper)
   1. Academic libraries--Aims and objectives--United States. 2. Academic libraries--United States--Sociological aspects. 3. Academic Libraries--Social aspects--United States. 4. Academic librarians--United States--Attitudes. 5. Academic librarians--Professional ethics--United States. 6. Libraries and colleges--United States. 7. Education, higher--Economic aspects--United States. 8. Dialectical materialism. I. Title.
   Z675.U5B285 2015
   027.70973--dc23
                        2015006745

Contents

Acknowledgements   vii

Chapter 1 Introduction: Dialectics and the Modern Capitalist Academic Library   1

Chapter 2 Understanding the MCAL Non-Dialectically   23

Chapter 3 Dialectical Material Monism as Alternative Way to Understand the MCAL   55

Chapter 4 The MCAL and Ideology   93

Chapter 5 The Counter-Hegemonic Academic Librarian   125

Chapter 6 The Transition of Quantity into Quality as a Tool for Counter-Hegemony   141

Chapter 7 Conclusions (and Beginnings)   149

Appendix: Resources for the Counter-Hegemonic Academic Librarian   157

Bibliography   171

About the Author   187

Index   191

Acknowledgements

There are many people without whom this book project would not have come to fruition, and I lack the space to thank them all. First and foremost, I want thank my family: Mitzi, Stella, and Irene. This book is for them. I am grateful to my parents, Cheryl, Steve, Karen, and Fred, for their support and patience. Lea Susan Engle provided me with much inspiration as a former co-worker, research collaborator, and as an example of a librarian that acts upon her convictions surrounding social justice issues. There are many librarians and library workers that I would like to thank for providing me with examples of engaged professionalism. Texas A&M University Libraries is replete with them, and I learned much from these people about how to get good work done in a social environment, central Texas, that is as far from Austin ideologically as it is nearby geographically. In particular, I would like to thank the TAMU Libraries Faculty Research Committee, Simona Tabacaru, Eric Hartnett, Stephanie Graves, and Suzanne Shurtz, for allowing me the opportunity to present my ideas at various TAMU Libraries research colloquia, and for helping to fund my travel to conference presentations. I am very grateful to Dr. Michael Kraft for acting as a sounding board for my ideas during this project.

Chapter 1

INTRODUCTION: DIALECTICS AND THE MODERN CAPITALIST ACADEMIC LIBRARY

The central thesis of this collection of meditations on the dialectical academic library is that the library writ large is a continuous blur of transformations characterized by complex internal interconnections and indeterminate external boundaries; a real world, materialist dialectics that one may observe, understand, and shape. The observation that the academic library is insistently mutable and interconnected should come as no great surprise to anybody who has ever worked in a library. This conclusion should also be no big revelation to those people who may have never even set foot in a library building. Any reasonably deliberate reflection upon simple observation of the academic library as an institution should result in this conclusion. It takes only a bit more reflection upon the inconstancy and interconnection of the academic library to abstract such an observation about impermanence from the library to all of human reality, and then to begin exploring how the library relates to this greater reality. When the study of change involves structure, strategy, and intellectual consideration, the theorist and practitioner, which I refer to in this book as the critical analyst (a singular concept that encompasses both terms), has the capacity to make future change that is meaningful and durable.

In this chapter, I first consider the shifting nature of the library. Following this, I identify the primary object of analysis for this book, the modern capitalist academic library (hereafter referred to as the MCAL). I then lay out the objectives for the remainder of the book, and I provide a brief description of its structure.

The Dynamic Nature of the Library (and the Librarian)

Dialectics is the arm of philosophy concerned with the implacable yet predictable transformation of reality. Such transformations may be swift or slow, they may be peaceful or violent, and they may occur over extended periods of time or in revolutionary fits and starts. At times, transformations may be retarded by opposing and reactionary forces, but change happens in spite of these impediments. When the critical analyst accepts and internalizes this basic tenet of continuous change, she is on the way to becoming a dialectical thinker as well as a dialectical actor. She is better able to look beyond the surface forms of reality to better understand its content, and she is better able to devise and implement strategies that change both this form and content.

The modern library is a kaleidoscope of innovation. The Biblioteca Alexandrina, also known as the New Library of Alexandria, advertises online that it is "much more than a library," with millions of books, an internet archive, four museums, a planetarium, a science exploratory for children, an interactive virtual reality environment, exhibitions, art galleries, and academic research centers.[1] This boast seems slight of substance, however, when one considers that the task of defining the library as a phenomenon is an ongoing intellectual project. The twentieth century, and the first two decades of the twenty-first, have placed the library's mercurial nature in bas-relief. For many present day library patrons, and particularly for those patrons who did not know the library before the advent of the World Wide Web, many of whom may see the web and the library as interchangeable things, the notion of what a library is has spilled far beyond its traditional boundaries.

---

1. Biblioteca Alexandrina, "About the Library," accessed November 15, 2014, http://www.bibalex.org/aboutus/overview_en.aspx.

Many phenomena relating to the academic library have shifted and been reorganized in both the professional and the popular social consciousness. Take, for instance, the fact that the geography of the academic library is no longer confined to the vicinity of the library building, as evidenced by the recent push towards distance learning in higher education. One result of such distance learning initiatives is that many public service librarians have increasingly fewer in-person encounters with members of their community. Due to the introduction of virtual reference cooperatives, patrons who use chat reference services may even interact with librarians that work at other institutions in different states. The sense of what a library's community is, as a result, is altering dramatically. At the same time that these changes have provided libraries with greater reach and expanded spheres of influence, one suspects that this technologically mediated distance has alienated information gatekeeper from information seeker. Concepts like library patron should also be seen as chimeric in nature. In the MCAL, library patron has been extended to include new or previously ignored groups with new needs, levels of expertise, means of access, and limitations on access. The ways in which patrons understand themselves, and the ways in which information professionals categorize them, do not sit still, and these fluctuating understandings impact the provision of library services to patrons. The failure on the part of information professionals to understand change and/or the professionals' reactionary responses towards shifting social realities may result in institutional and professional stagnation. For example, some academic librarians work in environments that are indifferent or sometimes even openly hostile to increasingly visible at-risk groups like the LGBT community. Librarians attached to some religiously affiliated schools, for example, may be pressured to ignore LGBT community needs when building collections or developing and implementing outreach programs, or these libraries' subject selectors may be expected to build and maintain library collections that contribute to a groups' marginalization and oppression.

The role of the library professional has also shifted, as evidenced by the invention of new terms like "information professional," the shift of

LIS programs towards broader "I-school" models, and the proliferation of new job titles like "metadata librarian" or "user experience librarian" at both academic and public libraries. Developments like these have done much to challenge the librarian stereotype of being "fussy old [women] of either sex, myopic and repressed, and brandishing or cowering behind a date-stamp and surrounded by an array of notices which forbid every human activity."[2] Nevertheless, at the same moment that these adjustments reshape conceptions of librarianship and open up a dizzying array of new career opportunities to those inclined towards working in library and information science (LIS) related jobs, fragmentation may also result in the pigeonholing of professional mindset due to an increasing amount of specialization in occupational scope. Even though Marx referred to factory workers when he wrote that the increasingly granular job specialization amongst laborers leads to workers' increasing social one-dimensionality,[3] it is not difficult to draw similar conclusions concerning the restrictions placed on occupational depth and professional identity when one considers the specialization and compartmentalization of intellectual laborers.

Rubin wrote that all of these recent environmental changes are disconcerting for many librarians, "in part because rapid change has not been an aspect that librarianship has generally had to deal with."[4] Although I disagree slightly with Rubin in that I think that librarians have been faced with rapid change since the industrial revolution, I certainly agree with him that the technological advances of the past half-century have added to the general anxiety levels of LIS professionals. Nevertheless, at the same time that academic librarians are confronted with ceaseless innovation and are, as a consequence, constantly reevaluating

---

2. Penny Cowell, "Not All in the Mind: The Virile Profession," *Library Review* 29, no. 3 (1980): 167. One instance of the changing idea of the librarian stereotype is the development of the "hipster librarian."

3. Karl Marx, *Capital: A Critique of the Political Economy*, vol. I., trans. Ben Fowkes (London: Penguin Books, 1976), 458.

4. Richard E. Rubin, *Foundations of Library and Information Science* (New York: Neal-Schuman, 2000), 351.

what libraries do and what libraries may become, they retain certain traditional, even mythic, associations concerning the MCAL's position as a sort of sociocultural bedrock.

Academic libraries exist in an ambivalent relationship with change. As catalysts and incubators of change, they are integral to the development of the physical and social sciences, branches of science comprised of disciplines concerned with the positive transformation of human cognitive and physical realities. Academic libraries also drive the arts and humanities, disciplines by which humans develop understandings of their past, present, and future selves. Within this societal (re)generative matrix, academic librarians serve as midwives sitting at the bedside of knowledge creation. In addition to facilitating scholarly communication as mediators of information, academic librarians are educators. Whether this latter function is accomplished through direct instructional contact or through developing and providing access to the library collections, which in turn develops students, it is an important process of both knowledge generation and social production.

Nevertheless, despite their being an incredible motive force, academic libraries are also effective at warding off change and containing transformation. This is the basic contradiction of libraries and librarianship, change versus stasis, and the contradiction that I will refer to frequently in the pages that follow. Besides driving the creation of human history, all libraries function to preserve the past, insuring the continuity of culture and society. As a result of this mandate, all librarians are, in a sense, the custodians of civilization. Therefore, as both mediators of knowledge creation and guardians of history, academic librarians have a responsibility to understand their roles as information professionals as deeply as possible, and they have a responsibility to use their advantaged positions as librarians to benefit both their constituencies and the general welfare of society.

The Object of Analysis: The MCAL

Today's academic librarians either live and work in a deeply ingrained social formation, neoliberal capitalism, or else they live and work in a social formation that is influenced by neoliberal capitalism. Neoliberalism, referred to alternatively as neo-capitalism, advanced capitalism, and late-capitalism, operates on the presupposition that human societies function best when they are aligned with ideas and practices that support the free-market, i.e., laissez-faire and supply-side economics. Neoliberalism is typically contrasted with societies having governments that are heavily involved in regulating, managing, or planning the (free-market or otherwise) economy, e.g., the Keynesian welfare state or state capitalist models of government like that of the former Soviet Union and the present day People's Republic of China.[5] Marx and Engels' writings provide an incisive critique of capitalism, a historical complex of relations that reorganizes society through the old social organization's "[…] annihilation, the transformation of the individualized and scattered means of production, the transformation, therefore, of the dwarf-like property of the many into the giant property of the few […]."[6] This social transformation has resulted in a system of relations of production actualized in differential social classes that normalizes the oppression of dominated, subaltern groups though the exploitation of their labor and the appropriation of the products of their labor. In Marx and Engel's day, capitalism was characterized by rapid industrialization and symptomized by the gross exploitation of workers. Neoliberal capitalism is differentiated from earlier capitalism by the development of multinational corporations, finance capital, and technocratic bureaucracies. The last few decades leading up to the present have also been marked by an expanding globalization that steadily subsumes all things to the interests of capital. Capitalism, of course, has positive ramifications.

---

5. *Encyclopædia Britannica Online*, s. v. "governance," accessed May 7, 2014, http://www.britannica.com/EBchecked/topic/1449402/governance.

6. Marx, *Capital*, 928.

Marx and Engels themselves applauded the immense productive force of capitalism in the first chapter of the *Communist Manifesto*.[7] The negative repercussions of modern capitalism, however, are heinous. These repercussions include a rabid corporate imperialism that targets and exploits developing countries (creating new subaltern classes and reserve armies of labor), increasingly frequent and severe economic crises, and widening inequality between haves and have-nots, i.e., those people that produce and those people that distribute what is produced. Even though today's haves and have-nots are not easily categorized into the proletariat/bourgeois polarization of Marx's times, having fragmented, class may still be conceived as consisting of relational constructs involving differential and unfairly distributed proximities to capital and power. Such fragmentation, particularly in the United States, strengthens capitalism's position by curbing the development of class consciousness.[8] And, if anything, class fragmentation illustrates capitalism's extraordinary capability to mystify existing social relations as a means of self-preservation.

Even though neoliberal capitalism is marked by glaring social inequality, high levels of insecurity and anxiety, and crises, the system is flexible enough to adjust to its crises so as not to collapse. Furthermore, neoliberal social formations are structured in such a way as to reproduce existing social divisions and to make these divisions appear as natural phenomena instead of as historically conditioned and developed social disunion. For instance, economic success in neoliberal economies is often reduced to being the result of some sort of innate human quality of character (e.g., human determination) as opposed to being a consequence of social and historical conditions.

Regardless of its resiliency, neoliberal capitalism's internal contradictions insure conflict, and any conflict bears the potential to result in fundamental changes to all involved elements. The detachment between

---

7. Karl Marx and Frederick Engels, "Manifesto of the Communist Party," in *Economic and Philosophic Manuscripts of 1844 and the Communist Manifesto*, trans. Martin Milligan (Amherst, NY: Prometheus Books), 214.

8. Erik Olin Wright, *Classes* (London: Verso, 1985), 279-280.

the material realities of the present historical totality and general perceptions of the MCAL as being somehow divorced from the larger political economy is incorrect. Even though MCALs are many times attached to not-for-profit institutions, they both embody and reproduce the social relations of the capitalist totality. They are an historical consequence at the same moment that they are an historical impetus. MCALs realize neoliberal capitalism's values through their relations with the greater capitalist society in which they are intrinsic components.

Evidence of the MCAL's spiritual alignment and supplication to the predominant neoliberal outlook is displayed by the steady torsion of higher education to conform itself to capitalist business models. More and more frequently the free market determines the priorities that universities and colleges must concentrate their energies on to be successful, to be competitive, and to expand. Even if a particular institution of higher education does not itself directly create capital, a university or college would be considered behindhand if it did not in some capacity *think business* when developing and implementing its operational model. Success within the current social formation—a success as dictated by the ideology of the dominant culture—results from such *thinking business*, i.e., from warily engaging in economic competition and providing consumers what they want at a rate dictated by free-market competition.[9]

The largest body of consumers of higher education is the students. What the majority of these consumers desire out of higher education, indeed, what they are taught to desire, is to minimize their time in school while maximizing their earning potential. To accomplish these goals effectively, capitalist relations infuse education with the system's axial drive towards expansion and restructure its goals to fit the designs and conventions of capitalism. Thus we see the incorporation in higher education of preoccupations with time management, the maximization of profits, and incestuous corporate cronyism and cross-pollination (that

---

9. Donald R. Stabile, *Economics, Competition, and Academia: An Intellectual History of Sophism versus Virtue* (Cheltanham, UK: Edward Elgar, 2007), 4-5.

is, acting as nursery clubs for industry) in a process which Slaughter and Rhoades described as

> [...] redrawing the boundaries between public and private sector, and [colleges and universities] favor boundaries that allow them to participate in a wide variety of market activities that enable them to generate external revenues. Corporations participate in this redrawing because the new boundaries move research closer to the market, allowing universities to act as industrial laboratories and subsidizing the cost of product development.[10]

Since success for educational institutions that ape business is measured largely through quantification and accumulation, qualitative values like creativity and critical thinking are subordinated to the maintenance of the economic bottom line, resulting in the shift from a "knowledge regime" that is based conceptually on serving the public good to a system that "values knowledge privatization and profit taking in which institutions, inventor faculty, and corporations have claims that come before those of the public."[11] Colleges and universities are, in fact, excellent terrain for generating profit. O'Donnell noted that higher education has retained a feudal structure in which what "is lost in autonomy and spontaneity is gained (we like to think) in assurance, control, consistency, and predictability,"[12] all of which are also factors for assuring success in a capitalist world characterized by market unpredictability. Recent scholarship has suggested that capitalism thrives under hierarchical, bureaucratic control structures,[13] and colleges and universities fit in well to this schema.

---

10. Sheila Slaughter and Gary Rhoades, *Academic Capitalism and the New Economy: Markets, State, and Higher Education* (Baltimore, MA: John Hopkins University Press, 2004), 27.

11. Ibid., 29.

12. James J. O'Donnell, *Avatars of the Word: From Papyrus to Cyberspace* (London: Harvard University Press, 1998), 37.

13. Ernesto Screpanti, "Capitalist Forms and the Essence of Capitalism," *Review of International Political Economy* 6, no. 1 (1999), 5-6.

The MCAL, which sits squarely at the center of academic life, even if this center is being increasingly realized in cyberspace as opposed to physical space and geographic location, has moved increasingly into the orbit of neoliberalism. As a result of its capitalist affiliation, the library may be seen as complicit, if unwittingly so, with a general transformation of culture and cultural products, such as knowledge, into neoliberal forms. Applying Francois Lyotard's theories of technology and commodification to information technology, Gane concluded that "as knowledge becomes a force of production it also becomes both a tool and object of economic and political power."[14] Viewing reality as a web of codetermining relations requires that we amend Gane's statement to read "as knowledge *increasingly* becomes a force of production it also *increasingly* becomes both a tool and object of economic and political power," which also points to the *increasing* culpability of the corporatizing MCAL in the process.

Since the later part of the twentieth century, the neoliberal transformation of colleges and universities has been reflected in the proliferation of literature aimed at turning colleges and universities into business ventures. Recent popular books in this mold include Tierney's *Building the Responsive Campus: Creating High Performance Colleges and Universities* and Knapp and Siegel's *The Business of Higher Education*, both of which promote capitalist business models.[15] The LIS community has also paid close attention to the issue, with a corpus of monographs and journal articles extolling the virtues of the corporatization of the academic library. It has become a widely held view within LIS that the business approach is needed to bring libraries of all sorts into the twenty-first century. In an address at Rider University, John Buschman said that

---

14. Nicholas Gane, "Computerized Capitalism: The Media Theory of Jean-François Lyotard," *Information, Communication & Society* 6, no. 3 (2003): 435.

15. William G. Tierney, *Building the Responsive Campus: Creating High Performance Colleges and Universities* (Thousand Oaks, CA: Sage, 1999); John C. Knapp and David J. Siegel, *The Business of Higher Education*, 3rd ed. (Santa Barbara, CA: Praeger, 2009).

Recently, a small cottage industry within librarianship has developed in the form of articles on the "discovery" of the success of plush, super-chain bookstore outlets (like Barnes & Noble) as a place to browse for and read books. In this scenario, bookstores are seen as more successful "competitors," and a key to their success is their more open and welcoming atmosphere. One article went so far as to suggest that Barnes & Noble's staffing and pay structure, the quasi-catalog of inventory control systems, and the "reference" knowledge of staff was in all ways more effective than libraries—and they have comfy chairs and sell good coffee to boot.[16]

In a 1998 issue of *American Libraries*, Coffman suggested that public libraries be run like chain bookstores, exhorting public librarians to "let them [library patrons] drink lattes."[17] The proliferation of Starbucks franchises opening up in academic libraries (my own place of work recently had one installed) suggests that they have eagerly embraced this strategy. While it is questionable whether such a strategy actually constitutes progress—any collection preservation librarian would argue vehemently against that contention—it displays the coercive power of capitalism to bring social institutions into correspondence with its operating ideologies.

Somewhat expectedly, there has been pushback in LIS to the corporatization of higher education. Wolff argued that the privatization of higher education has had major negative consequences, resulting in rising costs that put college education out of the reach of many people, rising debt levels for those students and their parents that do decide to continue school, the exploitation of academic laborers, and disparities between the quality of private and public education.[18] Rochell noted the connection between advances in information technology and the increasing commodification of information and subsequent development of the

---

16. John Buschman, "On Libraries and the Public Sphere," *Library Philosophy and Practice* 7, no. 2 (Spring, 2005), http://www.webpages.uidaho.edu/~mbolin/buschman.htm.

17. Steve Coffman, "What if You Ran Your Library Like a Bookstore," *American Libraries* 29, no. 3 (March 1998): 46.

18. Richard D. Wolff, *Capitalism Hits the Fan: The Global Economic Meltdown and What to Do about It*, Updated ed. (Northampton, MA: Olive Branch Press, 2013), 25-31.

expanding "knowledge industry."[19] Bales argued that one result of this commodification is the double exploitation of the academic researchers attached to colleges and universities because of higher education's close association with for-profit publishing entities like Elsevier.[20] While much of the blame for these adversities may be placed on the doorstep of neoliberal capitalism as an overarching, ideologically insidious (in that it deftly insinuates itself as being "natural" to reality through both the formal and informal educational processes and a general immersion through culture) and imperialistic system, one must also wonder if the conscious adoption of neoliberal capitalist business models for education has exacerbated these problems. Ball, for instance, warned how the modern universities' obsession with productivity and evaluation, two inamoratas of neoliberalism and bases for a culture of performativity, threatens to debase educational and research practices:

> There is for many in Higher Education a growing sense of ontological insecurity: both a loss of a sense of meaning in what we do and of what is important in what we do. Are we doing things for the 'right' reasons, and how can we know! The first order effect of [neoliberal] performativity is to re-orient pedagogical and scholarly activities towards those which are likely to have a positive impact on measurable performance outcome and are a deflection of attention away from aspects of social, emotional or moral development that have no immediate measurable performative value.[21]

Writing about the present situation of higher education in New Zealand, Roberts argued that, while the neoliberal transformation of higher education may hold onto the language of quality over quantity, neoliberalism privileges the quantification of performance over values traditionally

---

19. Carlton Rochelle, "The Knowledge Business: Economic Issues of Access to Bibliographic Information," *College & Research Libraries* 46, no. 1 (1985): 5-12.

20. Stephen Bales, "Occupy Elsevier," *Information for Social Change* 32 (Summer/Autumn 2012): 7-9, http://libr.org/isc/issues/ISC32/ISC32.pdf.

21. Stephen J. Ball, "Performativity, Commodification and Commitment: An I-Spy Guide to the Neoliberal University," *British Journal of Educational Studies* 60, no. 1 (2012): 20.

associated with academic knowledge creation.[22] This concern over the commodification of higher education is not limited only to materialists, but can be found also in idealist admonitions against the present "Barnes and Nobleization" of education. Lamenting what he sees as the corporatization of Seneca College in King City, Ontario, Doughty opined that "learning at Seneca is noisy; it is not meditative. Language at Seneca is vulgar; it is not holy. Freedom at Seneca is mocked; it is not cherished, nor is it used. This is because quiet, and language and freedom do not serve corporate interests."[23] These complaints appear to be based in idealistic notions of education; nonetheless, they show a concern with the status quo that stretches across philosophical divides.

In LIS, this growing resistance to neoliberal capitalism is frequently carried out in print, which suggests that library professionals are both conscious of the MCAL's shifting and problematic relationship with its shifting and problematic social formation, and that they are also starting to realize that neoliberalism is a social formation that is ultimately malleable and not unchangeably essential. That is, if the MCAL can be brought into increasing conformation with a social formation, why can't social formations be modified by the work done within, and the work done to, the MCAL? Progressive action in academic libraries, work that in some way aims to curb or subvert the tide of neoliberalism in the interest of social justice, has existed for some time. For instance, in the late 1960s, American librarians fought to include alternative press materials, which often pushed for progressive social change or advanced radical political agendas, in their institutions' collections.[24] Initiatives like these marked the growing social consciousness among

---

22. Peter Roberts, "Neoliberalism, Performativity and Research," *Review of Education* 53, no. 4 (2007): 359.

23. Howard A. Doughty, "Steps to the Corporate Classroom: A Propositional Inventory," *College Quarterly* 11, no. 4 (2008), http://www.collegequarterly.ca/2008-vol11-num04-fall/doughty.html.

24. Toni Samek, *Intellectual Freedom and Social Responsibility in American Librarianship, 1967-1974* (Jefferson, NC: McFarland & Company, 2001), 38.

the profession.²⁵ In 1971, Lowenthal's seminal *Library Journal* article, "A Healthy Anger," connected the burgeoning feminist movement with librarianship, questioning the structure of a system in which women are the plebeians and men are the patricians.²⁶ The increasing recognition among professionals of the capitalist structures underlying the MCAL is a heartening development.

Nevertheless, at the same moment that the MCAL champions ideas with clear progressive content, it has remained a fundamentally socially conservative entity. Just as capitalist economies institute regulatory measures to control the motion and stasis of capitalism to prevent crises that may threaten the underlying structure of the system itself, the MCAL employs strategies to "move society forward" while protecting the status quo and their own interests as capitalist institutions. They may engage in these projects either overtly or cryptically.²⁷

Goals of This Book

With no apparent appeal to irony, American library pioneer Charles Cotton Dana wrote in 1912 that

> The workshop, the factory, the office building, the modern business of almost any kind, these, rather than the palace, the temple, the cathedral, the memorial hall, or the mortuary pile, however grand, supply the

---

25. Ibid.

26. Helen Lowenthal, "A Healthy Anger," *Library Journal* (1 September, 1971): 2598.

27. In John Buschman, Mark Rosenzweig, and Elaine Harger, "The Clear Imperative for Involvement: Librarians Must Address Social Issues," *American Libraries* 25, no. 6 (1994): 575, the authors pointed out a blatant manifestation of this contradiction in a 1993 ACRL policy statement: "Perhaps the most significant example of [the reactionary backlash by academic libraries] occurred last spring when ALA's Association of College and Research Libraries (ACRL) passed a policy that acknowledges that academic libraries are 'inextricably linked to the social, political, and economic fabric in which they exist,' yet goes on to state that ACRL should only act when social issues relate 'directly' to its mission and strategic plan, where ACRL is clearly recognized as the authority on the subject, and where fundamental professional issues are in question."

examples in general accordance with which the modern book laboratory should be constructed.[28]

Cotton was prescient about the library's correspondence to business models. Many librarians do not openly question the structural basis of the professional decision making that they engage in. This reticence may be because they rationalize away the corporatization of the library as a necessary evil of the capitalist world in which they live. They may feel the need to suppress their opposition because of their workplace culture. They may have a tenuous employment status (such as being untenured). Although being a politically conscious, progressive academic is ostensibly protected in many—but by no means all—U.S. colleges and universities by rules governing academic and intellectual freedom, non-dominant ideas still invite suspicion and retribution. The weak position that leftist academics are placed in is further undercut by neoliberal capitalism's imperialist tendencies to expand its markets. Not only does capitalism's drive to subsume new markets extend beyond national borders, it aligns its internal elements, including higher education and the library, to its interests.

Academic librarians chafe at the insinuation that the library is a capitalist apparatus, that it is used to reproduce inequality and oppression. I suspect that even those librarians who self-identify as being fiscally and/or socially conservative see such accusations as tawdry. Being attached to a powerful social institution, academic librarians have the potential to make modern life more fair and equitable for everyone that they affect, and I hold that a dialectical understanding of the academic library should bring one to the conclusion that everyone means literally *everyone*, i.e., everyone living on Earth, now and in the future. Many librarians, however, choose to ignore the sociopolitical implications of where they work and what they do at their jobs, possibly out of naiveté, cynicism, or an aversion to or distrust of "utopian" thinking (a word that has unfortunately taken on pejorative connotations). By "drawing the magic

---

28. John Cotton Dana, *Libraries: Addresses and Essays* (White Plains, NY: H.W. Wilson Company, 1916), 22.

cap down over [their] ears so as to deny that there are any monsters,"[29] such librarians have reduced themselves to being components of the academic library qua static social institution, instead of as catalysts for the library as a phenomenon that is constantly in the act of becoming. The decision to become an academic librarian, therefore, is inherently a political one. I hold that academic librarians have both the moral and rational imperative to work for social justice and towards ultimately utopian goals. *The Dialectic of Academic Librarianship* is written for those academic librarians who have chosen to work consciously for progressive change. I advocate that academic librarians systematically reflect on their profession by means of dialectical materialism, a philosophy most often associated with the theoretical work of Marx. Materialist dialectics offers a framework for understanding the changing academic library, and it is a valuable means for directing intellectual labor towards normative goals.

John Budd, a prominent LIS social theorist, wrote that "evolution happens, but the evolution of librarianship should be intentional, guided by professionals who are cognizant of and sensitive to the world in which librarianship exists… and will exist."[30] This book aims to support this aspiration by, as noted above, advocating for a strategic approach to change. To do this, I promote a somewhat unconventional but pedigreed Marxist approach to dialectical materialism, dialectical material monism, as a tool for the study and transformation of the academic library and, by extension, the social milieu in which it operates. I consider such heterodoxy to be justified. Nonconformist and heterodox thought has a long history in critical theory and cultural analysis, and elements of dialectical material monism are found throughout the history of heterodox Marxist theory.

Dialectics, therefore, is a way of navigating reality that is both liberating and empowering. The dialectician does not, however, have an easy

---

29. Marx, *Capital*, 91.

30. John M. Budd, *Self-Examination: The Present and Future of Librarianship* (Westport, CT: Libraries Unlimited, 2008), xiii.

journey ahead of her. Her path requires that she constantly question people's comfortable realities and the underlying assumptions that support these realities, and her ultimate goal is to fundamentally change these realities. Even mildly negative appraisals of the status quo can upset people who are content with their present situations. Change can be frightening, and those people who actively work towards affecting progressive change, particularly if they are professionals working in powerful social institutions such as the academic library, may become the targets of verbal vitriol and even physical violence.

The essays in this short book are a critique of the MCAL and are meant to serve as instruments for supporting a progressive and transformative professional praxis that consciously struggles against the dehumanizing aspects of neoliberal capitalism. I am mindful of the often treacherous history that surrounds philosophical sparring, and I harbor no illusions that the philosophical positions presented in this book will transform all readers into diehard Marxists and dialectical materialists. There is far too much bias against both dialectical and historical materialism for that to be a realistic expectation. Blind conversions are, in fact, antithetical to the underlying spirit of dialectical thinking, and it is not my intention to sign up new party members. The reader determines the ultimate meaning of this book as much as, if not more so, than the author, and this is where my hopes as an author lie. Synthesis is the most valuable element of intellectual growth, even if the end result of synthesis is but the reaffirmation of currently held beliefs in the light of the presented arguments.

Therefore, regardless of the reader's personal socio-political views, she should make the attempt to approach this text dialectically by entering into a constructive dialogue with its ideas. I believe that the library profession is very capable of engaging in a deep reflection on itself. This book calls for continuous reflection as an act of professional engagement, and I present reflection as an integral component of the academic librarian's practice. Indeed, reflection as a generative act is the academic librarian's practice; they traverse the information landscape for the purpose of understanding and altering a shared human landscape, and they are most effective when they consciously perform this task.

The Structure of the Book

In addition to this introductory chapter, *The Dialectic of Academic Librarianship* contains six further chapters and an appendix. Each chapter addresses specific elements of the materialist dialectic and applies or relates them back to the neoliberal MCAL. The book's chapters may be regarded as individual essays. Because of this design, I reiterate important concepts when necessary to facilitate non-linear readings of the book. Nonetheless, I have sequenced the chapters to provide the text with a conceptual flow. That is, the topical focus shifts from theory (chapters 2, 3, and 4) towards theory's application by means of professional practice (chapters 5 and 6). Following this conceptualization and analysis as a site of change, I investigate how the MCAL, operating as a conservative ideological institution, works against this continuous dialectical movement even though it is conceived as an integral part of this dialectical motion. Finally, I ask two questions: how do academic librarians fit into this milieu, and how should they fit into it? I conclude that the conscientious academic librarian should be a counter-hegemonic academic librarian. More specifically, the chapters are presented as follows:

Following this introduction, chapter 2, *Understanding the MCAL Non-Dialectically*, examines the traditional ways in which the MCAL is understood and studied. The chapter focuses on two epistemological approaches to viewing the MCAL: non-dialectical objective idealism and non-dialectical materialism. The discussion raises objections to both of these approaches in order to offer dialectical materialism as a viable alternative. I then introduce my reading of dialectical materialism, dialectical material monism, as a "cosmic" ontological and epistemological approach that embraces the idea of the unity of reality and its incessant flux.

Chapter 3, *Dialectical Material Monism as a Vehicle for Understanding the MCAL in Flux*, further investigates dialectical materialism as an alternative to static ways of understanding the MCAL. Dialectical material monism is a viable means for understanding both libraries and librarianship as dynamic phenomena, and offers an alternative to understandings of the institution and profession as a fixed or eternal entity. It allows for an organic conception of both physical and mental phenomena, explaining them both historically and in terms of the totalizing social reality in which we exist. I consider the intellectual history of the philosophy, look at the current conception of dialectical materialism in LIS, and then argue that this approach to LIS is an effective way to understand and transform the MCAL as a social institution.

Chapter 4, *The MCAL and Ideology*, addresses the question of the MCAL's apparent stability in light of the preceding chapter's discussion of library qua dialectical motion. Doing this allows us to understand the MCAL as an ideological instrument and an apparatus for social reproduction. The library is considered as an ideological tool throughout its history. I argue how the institution works as a motor for driving prevailing modes of society (e.g., feudalism, capitalism), and I reference various theories of ideology to explain this institutional intransigency.

Chapter 5, The Counter-Hegemonic Academic Librarian, presents the idea of the counter-hegemonic librarian, i.e., the theoretically conscious and politically aligned transformative academic librarian who acts as an agent for progressive change in the MCAL and, as a result, the larger capitalist society. This chapter identifies practicing academic librarians as candidates for driving the shift necessary to make academic libraries counter-hegemonic tools by acting as interventions against the MCAL's function as ideological state apparatuses. The argument draws upon the work of thinkers such as Gramsci, Freire, and Raber. Attached to the end of this chapter are two appendices.

Chapter 6, *The Transition of Quantity into Quality as a Tool for Counter-Hegemony*, suggests how a particular understanding of dialectical motion may be a useful tool for the counter-hegemonic librarian..

Chapter 7, *Conclusions (and Beginnings)*, acknowledges that there is much work to be done in transforming an MCAL. I advocate maintaining an optimistic approach to progressive library counter-hegemony and close with an appeal for the continued development of LIS as a normative science and politically informed practice.

The appendix, *Resources for Counter-Hegemonic-Academic Librarians*, provides annotated lists of valuable resources for counter-hegemonic librarians. These lists include: (1) recommended literature regarding dialectical materialism, (2) recommended LIS literature, (3) progressive organizations of use to the counter-hegemonic academic librarian, and (4) online resources for counter-hegemonic librarians.

A Note before Continuing

Unless otherwise specified, I use the acronym MCAL (i.e., modern capitalist academic library) to refer to the main object of analysis, which includes the modern capitalist academic library as an institution (e.g., the physical buildings and resources, relations of production, the interplay of ideas, as well as the idea of the library itself), people that use or are affected by the library, academic librarians as entities within this institution, and academic librarianship as a profession. Whether one takes a dialectical approach or a common sense approach to the MCAL, all of these things are necessary elements of each other and may not exist apart.

Second, as is obvious from the title of this book, I have chosen to focus principally on academic libraries and academic librarianship. I also concentrate on those academic libraries and librarians operating in the United States of America. I did this because I am an academic librarian currently practicing in an American MCAL, Texas A&M University Libraries, where I work as a subject liaison in humanities and social sciences. As an academic librarian at a U.S. public university library, I feel sufficiently imbedded in the sociocultural, political, and historical contexts of the U.S. MCAL to offer a valuable insider critique that is also introspective. Having now worked at Texas A&M Libraries for six years, I am personally invested in the MCAL as an institution. I feel a responsibility to the communities that I serve, as well as to the segments of larger society that fall under the MCAL's influence and encounter its effects, as well as impact it. Narrowing my analysis to academic libraries and librarianship in neoliberal societies, and primarily to those academic libraries in the U.S., also makes the task at hand more manageable. Nevertheless, the arguments made and conclusions drawn may certainly be applied to other sorts of libraries in the United States and other countries. Considering the nature of the dialectical views that I espouse, such applications are necessary.

Chapter 2

UNDERSTANDING THE MCAL NON-DIALECTICALLY

Librarians have long sought to define both the library and their profession. It seems impossible, however, to pin down either the library as an institution or librarianship. The task is ultimately quixotic because the library, in its many different historical manifestations, embodies multiple meanings and modalities that slip and shift in relationship to the constellations of things that comprise human existence and experience and that make our total reality. Within this all-encompassing total reality, the academic library may be viewed in many different ways, three possible modes of orientation being the following: (1) ultimate reality as a fixed concept or collection of fixed concepts, (2) ultimate reality as a fixed objective material presence, and as I contend in this book, (3) ultimate reality as the material interaction of both mental concepts and physical objects as they mesh together in human culture and history as material presence.

Assuming any one of these perspectives affects how academic librarians engage in their theoretical approach to LIS and their professional praxis, thus undergirding their professional agency when interpreting and shaping the field. I propose the conscious application of theory as a remedy for professional inertia. Carefully considering what we do, why we do it, and where our professional lives take us and everybody else is needed for the realization of productive change both within and beyond the MCAL. Acting otherwise, or not-acting at all, reduces the academic librarian to something like a clerk or a bureaucratic functionary. This chapter considers two non-dialectical approaches, non-dialectical objective idealism and non-dialectical materialism, both of which have traditionally been employed in the capitalist social formation to make sense of what we perceive as the "not us." It looks at how these approaches contribute to how we navigate the MCAL. I then introduce dialectical materialism as an alternative.

Non-Dialectical Objective Idealism

Before proceeding, it is important to note that there is a difference between theoretical idealism and practical idealism. Bukharin wrote that while theoretical idealism is a commitment taken towards an ontological position concerning the elevation of ideas over matter, anyone who maintains a theoretical position of any sort is a practical idealist. Dialectical materialists are idealists in the practical sense even if they "may be an outspoken opponent of philosophical idealism, of theoretical idealism."[1] Dialectical materialists must be idealists in this sense.

According to the *Encyclopedia of Philosophy*, theoretical idealism is "the view that mind and spiritual values are fundamental in the world as a whole."[2] Idealism has long been a major current in Western philosophy and is seen as being opposed to both naturalism and realism.[3] Marxian theorists have criticized idealism as being rooted in the structures of class society and bearing some responsibility for perpetuating the material conditions of human society.[4] There are many different theoretical variations of idealism, but they may be crudely subdivided into two basic camps: (1) objective idealism (the belief in the objective existence of ideas above and beyond physical existence) and (2) subjective or empirical idealism (the belief in the primacy of one's own mind and

---

1. Nikolai Bukharin, *Historical Materialism: A System of Sociology* (Mansfield Centre, CT: Martino Publishing, 2013), 57.

2. H.B. Acton, "Idealism," *Encyclopedia of Philosophy*, vol. 4., ed. Paul Edwards (New York: Macmillan, 1967), 110.

3. Ibid.

4. Ira Gollobin, *Dialectical Materialism: Its Laws, Categories, and Practice* (New York: Petras Press, 1986), 60.

consciousness). This essay focuses on non-dialectical objective idealism (there are also dialectical approaches to idealism, exemplified in Hegelianism, but such approaches have a waning impact on both modern philosophical views and the more general *Weltanschauung*). This idealistic philosophical frame of reference, if not undisguised in its presence in the MCAL, permeates our relationships with the institution.

Objective idealism maintains that ideas exist apart from and prior to matter. The archetypal exposition of this philosophy is Plato's theory of forms, that physical phenomena reflect transcendent, indivisible, and eternal forms that are antecedent and superior to transient physical manifestations, the latter being pale reflections of the former. Possibly the most prevalent form of philosophical idealism found in modern capitalist society, particularly in the U.S., is religious monotheism and the belief in an eternal deity that exists apart from the physical world and that is ultimately responsible for its existence. A valid criticism of objective idealism is that it is disconnected from human history, for ultimate ideas are removed from impermanent historical circumstances. Understanding objective truth as something apart from and ultimately above a fluctuating physical existence potentially cheapens physical existence and alienates humans from the characteristics of their material existence. Feuerbach identified this alienation in his explanation of religion as the projection of human characteristics onto the form of a deity, where "God, as a metaphysical being, is the intelligence satisfied in itself, or rather, conversely, the intelligence, satisfied in itself, thinking itself as the absolute being, is God as a metaphysical being."[5]

Dialectical materialists have a problem with metaphysics, or at least metaphysics as they understand it in a specific manner. Nonetheless, all philosophies have some sort of metaphysical component, including positivism and dialectical materialism, because all philosophies contain some assumptions or arguments that are held *a priori* or go beyond empirical experience. The particular argument for dialectical materialism

---

5. Ludwig Feuerbach, *The Essence of Christianity*, trans. George Eliot (New York: Harper & Brothers, 1957), 37.

in the following chapters, for instance, rests on a Spinozist metaphysics that maintains a monist argument concerning the ultimate unity of reality. Theoretical idealism is particularly noxious in its abuse of the metaphysical. By putting ideas prior to and above matter, as well as its tendency to elevate rationalism over experience, it often lapses into speculation that invites accusations of religious and mystical thinking. Much of this speculative thought is untestable and indemonstrable and is relatively easy for materialists of all stripes to refute.

Idealism provides concepts with a sort of eternal status, as existing both within themselves and independently apart from other things. A frequent consequence of objective idealism being so ingrained within the Western culture and psyche is that ideas become either explicitly or implicitly turned into Big T Truths that are seen to exist as objective and eternal truths (hereafter, Big T Truths will be identified by capitalization, while contextual "truths" will remain uncapitalized). Examples include Human Nature, Love, or God. Such truths, one discovers, can lead to turgidity, and this stagnation is reflected in and repeated by the structures that comprise society and culture. Chapter 1 briefly introduced the notion that ideas may be turned into simplistic abstractions and that this is a risk when idealisms are not subjected to careful criticism. Ideas can be fixed, whether this is done intentionally or otherwise, in ways that make them resistant to both criticism and change.

In Stefan Zweig's 1939 novel *Beware of Pity*, Hofmiller, the story's protagonist, decries the asininity that he sees coming as a result of the uncritical adherence to grand abstractions like Patriotism and Honor. In the process of venting his frustration, he shows his ability to think critically, to question and look behind our received Truths:

> During the war [World War I] practically the only courage I came across was mass courage, the courage that comes of being one of a herd, and anyone who examines this phenomenon more closely will find it to be compounded of some very strange elements: a great deal of vanity, a great deal of recklessness and even boredom, but, above all a great deal of fear—yes, fear of staying behind, fear of being

sneered at, fear of independent action, and fear, above all, of taking a stand against the mass enthusiasm of one's fellows.[6]

In this passage, Hofmiller expresses his disgust for blind compulsion towards war as well as the acquiescence of people drawn into conflict and death because of the convergence of political power and "eternal" sociocultural ideas like Patriotism. In this book, I aim to show that such complacency is limited not only to those people swept up by explicitly formulated, dogmatic, and sometimes even dangerous ideologies (e.g., National Socialism, Stalinist communism/state capitalism, bureaucratic socialism). The reluctance to take a stand also results from human groups' exposure to embedded institutions of society, even those institutions, like the academic library, that we tend to consider as wholly benign.

The MCAL Seen through the Big T Truths of Non-Dialectical Objective Idealism

As an assemblage of concepts, the MCAL is a network of abstract ideas and structured ideologies that, to varying degrees, we either implicitly hold or explicitly acknowledge. Academic librarians are familiar with abstract clichés like Knowledge is Power, but how often do they critically analyze such adages in relation to themselves and where they work? If they are considered in isolation from the entirety of material reality, ideas about the library have the potential to be reduced to one-sided abstractions such as Storehouse of Knowledge, Universal Library, and Conservator of Order.[7] Simplistic abstractions, therefore, are objective idealisms that stealthily contribute to the fixing of the structural character of the academic library, and in the process make this character seem eternal. Such a capitalist ideological structure manifests itself in an

---

6. Stefan Zwieg, *Beware of Pity*, trans. Phyllis and Trevor Blewitt (New York: New York Review Books, 2006), xxxii.

7. Michael H. Harris, "The Role of the Public Library in American Life," *University of Illinois Graduate School of Library Science Occasional Papers*, no. 117 (1972): 8.

MCAL that Knapp described in a way that effectively highlights these abstractions within their capitalist contextual milieu:

> [...] [The modern academic library] is dominated by the rational-bureaucratic model, modified somewhat by certain values to which we adhere in what is often a sentimental rather than a realistic fashion. Thus a "good" administration is one in which matters of authority and responsibility are clear-cut and well-defined, activities are performed in accordance with uniform standards, procedures are codified, performance is evaluated by means of objective measures of cost and efficiency. The "good" administrator achieves all this, of course, with due regard for the individual rights and "human" feelings of the personnel.[8]

In this excerpt, Knapp presents several abstract ideas which support the successful realization of the "rational-bureaucratic" MCAL within the greater capitalist social totality as a locus for realizing free market-based economic costs. As historically situated (i.e., neoliberal capitalist) concepts, these terms may be translated into the abstractions "clear-cut and well defined [hierarchies]," "uniform standards [of possible action]," "codified procedures," "objective measures," "efficiency," "individual [human] rights," and "human feelings." Knapp's analysis is perceptive in that she identifies these ideas as "values to which we adhere in what is often a sentimental rather than a realistic fashion."[9] Certain keywords that she uses, like Good and Human Feelings, are tied to our conceptions about the places where librarians work, as are other abstract and lofty concepts like Intellectual Freedom. Critical analysts of the present U.S. MCAL, however, may take cheer. With its adoption of business models and terminology, this MCAL is more transparent than its predecessors, increasingly wearing its ideology on its sleeve.

---

8. Patricia A. Knapp, "The Library as a Complex Organization: Implications for Library Education," in *Towards a Theory of Librarianship: Papers in Honor of Jesse Hauk Shera*, ed. Conrad H. Rawski (Metuchen, NJ: Scarecrow Press, 1973), 488-489.

9. Ibid., 488.

Abstractions, while necessary for analytical thought, become lacking in meaning when, as Ollman wrote, they have "lost touch with all human specificity" and are rendered simplistic when their "ties with the rest [of reality] are not apparent."[10] Whether or not we are aware that we are approaching reality like this, objective idealism is a common trap for most every librarian, me included. It presupposes some, usually romantic, archetype of the MCAL and proposes that the material MCAL does or should conform to this expectation, resulting in a gulf between the cognition of material stuff and ideal stuff. The concrete understanding of what engendered the MCAL, the form and nature of the current institution, and where the institution may be heading, are replaced with a vision of the MCAL as absolute. Librarians' core professional aims typically revolve around such simplistic abstractions, ideas like Human Progress, Freedom, and Democracy. Complicating matters, academic librarians are many times not fully aware of how material reality may run contrary to simplistic abstractions, and how contradictions within this reality obviate attempts at achieving these abstracted goals. In *Our Enduring Values: Librarianship in the 21st Century*, Michael Gorman identified Eight Central Values of Librarianship: (1) Stewardship, (2) Service, (3) Intellectual Freedom, (4) Privacy, (5) Rationalism, (6) Commitment to Literacy and Learning, (7) Equity of Access, and (8) Democracy.[11] He wrote that these values should not be viewed as absolutes, but as "standards by which we assess what we do; measure how near we are to, or how far we are from, an objective; and compare our actions and our state of being to those of others to the ideals represented by our values."[12] Gorman understood that values such as his Eight Central Values may indeed become absolutes and that absolutes are counterproductive because they stop discussion.

---

10. Bertell Ollman, *Alienation: Marx's Conception of Man in Capitalist Society* (London: Cambridge University Press, 1971), 134.

11. Michael Gorman, *Our Enduring Values: Librarianship in the 21st Century* (Chicago, IL: American Library Association, 2000).

12. Ibid., 7.

If you hold up any set of values to the light of the realities of neoliberal capitalism, they may be seen as emanating from capitalism at the same time that they seem to countermand many aspects of capitalism. Analysis of such conflicts reveals the exploitative power relationships of capitalism that sometimes lead to the co-option and contradiction of the spirit of such concepts to create, as Gorman wrote, distorted value systems.[13] As a result, the Big T Truths should be understood as organic to the particular historical contexts in which they are situated and not as objective ideals. Enright, for instance, noted that educational initiatives enacted by the Australian government worked to see that "the ideology of lifelong learning is deployed so as to ensure the widespread and perpetual re-training of the labor force so as to continue to compete in a global economy characterized by the rapid emergence of new information technologies."[14] This logic appears repeatedly in both written government policy and in statements by government officials.[15] This capitalist market iteration and enshrinement in government policy of Gorman's Central Value of Commitment to Literacy and Learning represents the twisting of a value to support the capitalist agenda.

This mode of thought persists in LIS and it always seems to connect back in some way to Democracy, the discipline's most sacrosanct Big T Truth. D'Angelo argued that public libraries are losing touch with their basic mission of supporting the public good, identifying this deviation as an effect of neoliberal, postmodern consumer capitalism.[16] He distinguished between the pre-postmodern public library and the present day, postmodern public library, with the latter libraries displaying an increasingly obvious market orientation that replaces "the citizen as the

---

13. Ibid.

14. Nathaniel F. Enright, "The Violence of Information Literacy: Neoliberalism and the Human as Capital," in *Information Literacy and Social Justice: Radical Professional Praxis*, eds. Lua Gregory and Shana Higgins (Sacramento, CA: Library Juice Press, 2013), 28.

15. Enright, "Violence of Information Literacy," 28-29.

16. Ed D'Angelo, *Barbarians at the Gates of the Public Library: How Postodern Consumer Capitalism Threatens Democracy, Civil Education and the Public Good* (Duluth, MN: Library Juice Press, 2006), 1-4.

primary agent of 'democracy' or what is being called democracy" with the consumer.[17] This distinction between democracy in its dialectical understanding and Big Democracy is a crucial one. Democracy is disingenuous in a genetic sense; it conceals its historically bound contents at the expense of the people that it directly affects. Democracy is a problematic idea that is removed from its historical context, and one that the critical analyst must be wary of. When located in its historical context, this Democracy may be seen as an Enlightenment and early capitalist iteration of an ever-shifting actuality that exists only in conjunction with actually existing material relations (democracy itself being a relation). Democracy is one understanding of contextual democracy that evolved out of the work of bourgeois philosophers like Rousseau and Locke, who both lived in early capitalist societies. Locke, for instance, wrote that the ownership of private property was a fundamental human right, a position that certainly influenced, and was influenced by, burgeoning social democratic ideas about what a proper understanding of such democracy entailed. The fact that capitalist Democracy remains for many people in the same largely uncontested form that it has existed in since the Enlightenment shows the human penchant for conflating ideological moments into cultural myths, narratives that work as effective tools for cultural conservation. These examples highlight people's habit of normalizing the actual. Prior to the postmodern library, the library patron was also integrated into the master set of social relations that comprised the developing capitalist social formation and codetermined "her" library. Her library also worked towards a democracy, but not Democracy in broad and abstract brushstrokes. Democracy is so abstract, in fact, that the word does not have to be defined to most Western readers. Just reading the word in context allows them to tap into a shared mythological narrative. American libraries, both public and academic, have always worked for democracy in some qualified sense, while they have always touted Democracy, and thus have always set themselves up for failure at achieving a goal that is ultimately absurd.

---

17. Ibid., 9.

Libraries everywhere, in fact, have always worked for some variation of democracy, whether it's the U.S. democracy, the Chinese democracy, the U.K. democracy, the Iranian democracy, capitalist democracy, or socialist democracy. If one neglects to consider qualifying prefixes, she risks slipping away from a thoroughgoing critique that sees the MCAL as enmeshed in history towards normalizing the actual, idealizing the past, and most likely doing both.

Diversity is another example of a simplistic abstraction that has become a watchword in higher education, and one that is increasingly being critiqued. Despite the blanket idealism associated with the term's modern usage, contemporary Diversity is the diversity of contemporary capitalism. It is formed out of relations found within the existing social structure. What is Diversity's function in the MCAL and to what extent is the idea reflected in the contextual reality of the MCAL? There is, for instance, a growing awareness among LIS professionals of "microaggressions" towards minority librarians that work within public and academic library work environments, despite the apotheosis of Diversity. Microaggressions are "brief, everyday exchanges that send denigrating messages to certain individuals because of their group membership (people of color, women, or LGBTs)"[18] They reinforce traditional structures of domination. Microaggressions gird the status quo through the sublimation of more overt maneuvering on the part of those in positions of dominance. That these actions regularly take place belies the material realities of the environment in which we work, and microaggressions both provide evidence for the progressivity of this environment (one in which the need for inclusivity has become more overt, resulting in discrimination having to resort to the covert) at the same time that they display capitalism's ability to adapt and hide its methods of control to perpetuate itself. Recently, several cutting-edge poster presentations regarding microaggressions and librarianship have appeared at national

---

18. Derald Wing Sue, *Microaggressions in Everyday Life: Race, Gender, and Sexual Orientation* (Hoboken, NJ: Wiley, 2010), 24.

LIS conferences, providing the phenomenon with much exposure.[19] A website, *Microaggressions in Librarianship*, was created to provide a space for library workers to anonymously post instances of microaggressions that left them feeling marginalized. Posts have documented microaggressions including: "Assigned to search committees because I'm the only Latina librarian," "Professors will talk slower to me after hearing my full name," and "After some ugly anti-LGBT incidents in our community, the library held LGBT ally training. It was mandatory for all librarians and staff—except for people who opted out due to 'personal beliefs.'"[20] Diversity is touted as beneficial to the MCAL because it is an apparently transcendent, morally exemplary ideal. But, at the same time, this is a capitalist iteration of Diversity that is bound to the political economy of that social formation and contributes to its economic success. This same Diversity, however, appears to be restrained in capitalism so as to maintain hierarchical structure and dominant interests, hence the use of microaggressions as corrective interventions. The Diversity of capitalism is co-defined by its relationship with the Equality of capitalism, an equality that is also ultimately subservient to capitalism's hierarchical and patriarchal structure. In her essay "Racial Capitalism," Nancy Leong described the commodification of race (one may also substitute gender or economic position for race) and race's subsequent exploitation as capital through things like diversity hiring by institutions of higher education. The dominant classes, what Leong said are composed of "generally white people and predominantly white institutions,"[21] derive value from engaging in diversity recruiting. Besides the obvious and

---

19. Jaena Alabi, "'Race is a Social Construct that does not Exist': What Librarians Have to Say about Racism in the Profession," (poster presented at the 2014 American Library Association Annual Conference, Las Vegas, 2014); Cynthia Mari Orozco, Elvia Arroyo-Ramirez, Rose L. Chou, and Anni Pho, "Increasing the Diversity Dialogue: Sharing Our Experiences with Microaggressions in Librarianship," (poster presented at the 2014 American Library Association Annual Conference, Las Vegas, 2014).

20. "Microaggressions in Librarianship," Microaggressions in Librarianship, accessed November 15, 2014, http://lismicroaggressions.tumblr.com.

21. Nancy Leong, "Racial Capitalism," *Harvard Law Review* 126, no. 8 (2013): 2191.

often repeated benefits of broadening an organization's knowledge base and increasing its capacity for innovation, such recruiting benefits the reputation of the organization and provides a statistical defense against litigation.[22] The institutionalization of Diversity measures within capitalist systems, however, operates to harvest the "racial capital" from minority group members, exploiting dominated portions of capitalist society in the same way they have been for centuries, as commodities.

Objective Idealisms have sometimes popped up in the LIS professional and research literature in an uncritical fashion. Maxwell's *Sacred Stacks: The Higher Purpose of Libraries and Librarianship* represents one such objective idealistic approach. Maxwell wrote in her preface that she "argues that libraries have survived, and will continue to thrive in the future, because they fulfill eternal needs for people."[23] These "eternal needs" suggest that people possess some type of unchanging, and therefore unprovable, requirements that transcend situation, and that the library does or should fulfill these needs regardless of individual culture or the defining socioeconomic relations of the era. And, if the material library does not fulfill this function, it may be held up as deficient when compared to the Library as an absolute idea. Maxwell also wrote about the library's "sacred" functions, comparing S.R. Ranganathan's *Five Laws of Librarianship* with Prothero's summarization of the underlying idealist beliefs of liberal Protestantism, summarized in table 1.

As with the Christian religious beliefs, formulations like Ranganathan's *Laws* may be viewed as *a priori* axioms; that is, they may be seen as existing in the mind prior to experience. The *Five Laws* are certainly noble and apparently benign pronouncements, but they betray their objective idealism in their absolutism. They take a contextually based reality and impose it as transcendent laws to be taught to LIS graduate students likely sans historical context and applicable regardless of the prevailing mode of production. Upon critique, simplistic abstractions

---

22. Ibid., 2195-2196.

23. Nancy Kalikow Maxwell, *Sacred Stacks: The Higher Purpose of Libraries and Librarianship* (Chicago, IL: American Library Association, 2006), viii.

Table 1

MAXWELL'S COMPARISON OF PROTHERO'S BASIC TENETS OF LIBERAL PROTESTANTISM WITH RANGANATHAN'S FIVE LAWS OF LIBRARIANSHIP[24]

Liberal Protestantism	*Ranganathan's Five Laws*
The goodness of humanity	Every reader his book
Inevitability of progress	Books are for use
	Save the time of the user
Necessity of good works	Every book its reader
Immanence of God in nature, culture, and the human heart.	Library is a growing organism

like Ranganathan's *Five Laws* may always eventually be tied to historical circumstance. The *Five Laws* were developed by a middle class academic in a developing capitalist-colonial country (twentieth century India) administrated by a capitalist social democracy (Great Britain). Therefore, it is not surprising that the *Five Laws* reflect bourgeois views concerning individuality such as "every reader his book" and "every book its reader," as well as capitalist concepts of private ownership. The very use of the male pronoun as the possessor half of the ownership relation in Ranganathan's formula points to the patriarchal capitalist system in which it developed. Considering the historical context in which it was written, the Third Law, "Save the time of the reader," might be decoded as "time is money." In the same instance that the *Five Laws* portray themselves as altruistic, natural "laws," they betray their orientation to a social formation that alienates and oppresses. A Sumerian scribe-priest of the second millennium BCE would have found Ranganathan's *Five Laws* alien to his understanding of librarianship, which, for the scribe, revolved around the maintenance of the state in the personage of the king, whose hereditary position had come to represent "the very hallmark

---

24. Ibid., 35.

of civilization."[25] To the scribe, laws such as "Every book its reader" and "Every reader its book" would have been essentially meaningless, because all of the tablets in his archive were the property of the state and the king. In fact, one Sumerian "law of librarianship," if they had such things, might have been to "maintain the welfare of the state in the personage of the king." Arguably, this so-called law has applied to the majority of societies for a large stretch of human history. Nonetheless, such concepts have been reformulated by material changes, as they will be again in the future. Economic and political processes that have taken place in India, for example, resulted in real world material change and the realignment of material relations. Ranganathan, as is the case with all human beings, was himself a product of these relations, as were his ideas concerning both information and individuality.

There are many more examples of how abstract ideas of the MCAL are misleading, how they are, in actuality, context bound and historically dependent. Abstractions like Democracy and Diversity inevitably surrender their transcendence when they are carefully interrogated and situated within a concrete network of phenomena that are more obviously grounded in historical context. A careful analysis of Diversity, Equality, or Democracy allows us see these things as being codetermined by phenomena and processes like institutionalized racism, colonialism, and the systemic commodification of all things that may be squeezed of exchange value. All of these phenomena are themselves codetermined by the contextual situation within which they sit—in this case, neoliberal capitalism. Non-dialectical objective idealism's ignoring of context and history renders the Big T Truths neutered of their historically based content and makes their internal conflicts invisible, at the same time that it supports their continued operation.

Finally, critical analysts of the MCAL should avoid the trap of conservative nostalgia for the past "less capitalist, more ideal" library. When argued from particular, often valid, perspectives, the current situation

---

25. Samuel Noah Kramer, *The Sumerians: Their History, Culture, and Character* (Chicago, IL: University of Chicago Press, 1963), 74.

appears dire for today's libraries. Social critics, however, sometimes magnify problems in relationship to an idealized past. We see this with Doughty's complaints, related in the previous chapter, but repeated here for the purpose of critique, that "language at Seneca is vulgar; it is not holy. Freedom at Seneca is mocked; it is not cherished, nor is it used. This is because quiet, and language and freedom do not serve corporate interests."[26] What exactly are Vulgarity, Holiness, and Freedom? How are things less Holy at Seneca now than in the past? The question is worth asking, particularly when one sees that Doughty made his statements while apparently assuming that his audience understood what he meant, that they are in agreement with him as to the content of a form that appears to transcend context completely. The capitalist social formation has shown itself adept at encouraging this type of thinking, which works to insure the structural survival of a social formation that is prone to crises.

The MCAL, like the factory, the machinery of popular culture, governmental institutions, and even the modern nuclear family, is a site of struggle within modern neoliberal capitalism. Despite the fact that capitalism is extraordinarily effective at masking this struggle, its veneer is threadbare in places, revealing the incoherencies found beneath the glossy surface idealisms, that is, in the contextual reality. If one adopts a Marxist view of society as divided by unequal competing classes, then such idealistic orderings of reality take on political hues, and the separation of mind from the physical (or even the complete dismissal of the existence of the latter) act as tools for maintaining, as Gorter wrote, the power of the ruling classes:

> The bourgeoisie want to convince the workers that mind is above material social existence, that mind alone rules and forms matter. They have been using mind as a means of domination: they have science, law, politics, art and the Church behind them and their rule incorporates all of these things. Now they want to make the workers believe that this is

---

26. Howard A. Doughty, "Steps to the Corporate Classroom: A Propositional Inventory," *College Quarterly* 11, no. 4 (2008), http://www.collegequarterly.ca/2008-vol11-num04-fall/doughty.html.

an expression of the natural order; that mind by its nature rules over material social existence, that it rules over the workers in the factory, the mine, the farm, the railroad and the ship. The worker who believes that mind creates production, labor and social classes by itself, this worker submits to the bourgeoisie and their accomplices, the priests, the experts, etc., because the bourgeoisie controls the majority of the sciences, it controls the Church, and thus mind, and, if this is true, it must rule.[27]

Although Gorter's conclusions show the hyperbole typical of early-twentieth century Marxist revolutionary writings, his accusation may still be applied to how dominant classes use idealistic conceptions of reality as a means of maintaining hegemonic control of a society. But idealism becomes farce when the source of the idealism both supports and is braced by a material reality that runs counter to the core values espoused by the idealist.

The transformational academic librarian must remain wary of both nostalgia and the Big Ideas. Libraries are part of the warp and woof of human history. Being a part of this history, they act as a major impetus for propelling history in either a progressive or reactionary fashion. They are inseparable from the continuous flow of history and they are bereft of any progressive consequence if they are considered apart from that history, becoming remote and drained of meaning.[28] Even if one dismisses the relevance of Hegelian or Marxist ideas concerning the primacy of historical social modes or structures, it is hard to deny that the current historical situation in which we find ourselves is characteristically distinct, that it has not always existed in quite the same socio-cultural and economic form, and that it will not necessarily, nor will it likely, remain in its current historical form, no matter how unquestioned and mythologized that form has become. This fundamental realization leads us also to the conclusion that there have actually been many different libraries over the course of human history and that these different libraries possessed different—and shifting—values, principles,

---

27. Herman Gorter, "Historical Materialism," Marxists.org, accessed January 2, 2014, https://www.marxists.org/archive/gorter/1920/historical-materialism.htm.

28. Bertell Ollman, *Alienation*, 134.

and philosophies. The MCAL is different now than it had once been in spite of any set of values. Values are in fact different from moment-to-moment, a realization that then requires us to understand why they exist as ideas and what role they perform in the MCAL. At the same time that these realizations help to knock the legs out from under reality as we understand it, they result in no small amount of existential anxiety. But the shift also reinforces the dialectical conception of reality and suggests that the human future reality can be qualitatively better than it is currently despite the unfortunate deficiencies that our analyses may uncover. Since academic librarians are usually very intelligent people who think critically about where they work, many become increasingly conscious of the inauthentic relationships between their set of received, traditional values concerning the MCAL and the material realities of the socio-cultural environment in which they navigate. Chapter 4 looks at the ideological fixing of hegemony in greater detail. But first, let us look at non-dialectical materialism, idealism's chief competitor, and sometimes its crony, for how we make sense of the capitalist world.

Non-Dialectical Materialism

Non-dialectical materialism, sometimes referred to by dialectical materialists as metaphysical materialism, is a way of understanding reality that is exemplified by post-Baconian science and the work of scientists and philosophers in the seventeenth and eighteenth centuries. Empirical science and its associated philosophies have traditionally espoused ideologies that strive to fix our understanding of the objects comprising the natural world and human society, and the forces that influence and regulate them. These systems place much emphasis on identifying and knowing the individual qua their essence and show little regard for either integrative understanding or historical development. Through observing and analyzing objects and forces, the non-dialectical materialist philosopher and/or scientist purports to gain an objective knowledge of reality that extends beyond a particular context to encompass the definitions and comprehension of individual, material phenomena. However, even when the objects of such an analysis are considered in relationship to each other, they are often treated in a serial, subordinated fashion. That is, the objects of science are evaluated in terms of physical cause and effect. Non-dialectical materialism imposes a materially-based understanding of reality upon an essentially static conception of history and truth, in the process often failing to adequately account for change, development, and socio-cultural habitus. Such a worldview has proven itself successful in the physical sciences, but concepts such as movement, development, and transformation—things of the utmost importance to dialecticians because they go a long way towards explaining the past, present, and future—are not as well-considered, or else they are given short shrift.

Non-dialectical materialism is the foundation upon which common sense and taken-for-granted ideas of what "proper" Science is rests. This philosophy of science has become closely related to notions of what constitutes legitimacy in knowledge creation and has become imbedded in Western culture in what Habermas termed as a "scientism," in which "Knowledge is implicitly defined by the achievement of the sciences," and "transcendental inquiry into the conditions of possible knowledge can be meaningfully pursued only in the form of methodological inquiry into the rules for the construction and corroboration of the scientific theories."[29] Such materialisms' scientistic manifestations are seen as recent developments, but they fulfill the same age-old functions as non-dialectical objective idealism. Pannekoek contended that what he called middle-class (i.e., capitalist or bourgeois) materialism substituted as an easy replacement for religion, the ultimate form of idealism:

> Among these [idealist] ideologies the least significant is religion. As with the withered husk of a system of ideas reflecting conditions of a far past, it has only an imaginary power as a refuge for all, who are frightened by capitalist development. Its basis has been continually undermined by capitalism itself. Middle-class philosophy then put in its place the belief in all these lesser idols, deified abstractions, such as matter, force,

---

29. Jürgen Habermas, *Knowledge and Human Interests*, trans. Jeremy J. Shapiro (Boston, MA: Beacon Press, 1971), 67.

causality in nature, liberty, and progress in society.[30]

Even though the dialectical materialists share with the non-dialectical materialists a basic understanding of reality as being grounded in material as opposed to mind or spirit, this does not exempt the non-dialectical approaches from being critiqued regarding their metaphysical positions. The modern usage of the term metaphysics, according to Krapivin, identifies the system of philosophy that "regards phenomena in isolation from each other and denies internal contradictions as the source of their development."[31] So dialectical materialists often use the term metaphysics in a pejorative sense when describing the shortcomings of the non-dialectical materialisms, where metaphysics means an untenable mode of thought in which boundaries are constructed around natural phenomena in order to fix them unnaturally. In his Anti-Dühring, Engels described this non-dialectical materialism as being a holdover from archaic ways of thinking about science:

> the habit of observing natural objects and natural processes in their isolation, detached from the whole vast interconnection of things; and therefore not in their motion, but in their repose; not as essentially changing, but as fixed constants; not in their life, but in their death. And when, as was the case with Bacon and Locke, this way of looking at things was transferred from natural science to philosophy, it produced the specific narrow-mindedness of the last centuries, the metaphysical mode of thought.[32]

Engels described non-dialectical materialism as the "science of things" as opposed to dialectics, the "science of movements."[33] This is an impor-

---

30. Anton Pannekoek, *Lenin as Philosopher: A Critical Examination of Philosophical Basis of Leninism*, rev. ed., ed. Lance Byron Richey (Milwaukee, WI: Marquette University Press, 2003), 159.

31. Vasilii Krapivin, *What is Dialectical Materialism?* (Moscow: Progress Publishers, 1985), 304.

32. Friedrich Engels, *Anti-Dühring: Herr Eugen Dühring's Revolution in Science*, ed. C.P. Dutt, trans. Emile Burns (New York: International Publishers, 1939), 36.

33. Frederick Engels, *Dialectics of Nature*, ed. and trans. Clemens Dutt (New

tant distinction to make, for, as we shall see with dialectical materialism, the concept "thing" folds into the concept "process," achieving a sort of flexibility of interpretation that challenges traditional views concerning existential boundaries and identities.

As with non-dialectical objective idealism, the concept of truth in non-dialectical materialist ontologies consists of the Big T Truth variety, i.e., that there exists truth waiting to be discovered by means of scientific inquiry, and this truth is objective and permanent. Engels described this standpoint as a vestigial metaphysics resulting in sciences that "busied themselves by inquiring into things as given in established quantities,"[34] an approach that "judges everything from the standpoint of the immediate motive,"[35] and treats the manifest state of reality as a final cause to be known as opposed to a transitory state within an eternally unfolding process. Take, for example, modern empirical scientific method's fixation on quantification and statistical procedures to generalize findings from a sample to a population, and which then puts forth positive epistemological positions and makes predictions based upon these positions. The positivist and post-positivist social sciences which dominate the academy in the U.S. tend to approach the objects of their study linearly in terms of cause and effect, that is, as completed entities. Such an approach becomes ingrained as tradition, be this tradition maintained through overt coercion or be it through its reification (i.e., its objectification or "thingification" as a corporal thing) in capitalist phenomena and institutions.[36] The MCAL represents one

---

York: International Publishers, 1940), 45.

34. Friedrich Engels. *Feuerbach—The Roots of the Socialist Philosophy*, trans. Austin Lewis (New York: Mondial, 2009), 72.

35. Ibid., 77-78.

36. Georg Lukacs wrote in *History and Class Consciousness: Studies in Marxist Dialectics*, trans. Rodney Livingstone (London: Merlin Press, 1971), 83, that reification was "The essence of the commodity-structure" and that its "basis is that a relation between people takes on the character of a thing and thus acquires a 'phantom objectivity', an autonomy that seems so strictly rational and all-embracing as to conceal every trace of its fundamental nature: the relation between people."

such instance of reification of a metaphysical worldview through its enshrinement as a temple to knowledge.[37]

The concept of the constant transformation of reality, however, seems intuitive to human beings. We all realize the reality of change on a gut level largely because we see it and live it. The necessity to account for change in both hard and social science, furthermore, began to appear in the nineteenth century, particularly with Darwin's theory of evolution, and of course in the social philosophy of Marx and Engels. For the most part however, with the exception of the followers of Marx and Engels, these realizations are underdeveloped and only tentatively used in approaching the MCAL.

The MCAL Seen through the Big S Science of Non-Dialectical Materialism

Although non-dialectical objective idealism impacts our understanding of the MCAL, it does so in a largely latent way. Non-dialectical materialism, on the other hand, is much more conspicuous in how it affects the ways in which people navigate the library because it has, in many ways, become the accepted systematic means for sense-making in the modern world, even if for many people non-dialectical materialism remains more of a taken-for-granted emblem of how the world works, both *de facto* and *du jour*, than it is a consciously applied method to problem solving and discovery.

One sign that non-dialectical materialism has a hold on the MCAL is the increasing popularity of disciplinary monikers like "library science" and "information science." Science, however, has become a loaded term. Where the word was once more simply understood as knowledge obtained in a particular branch of learning through methodological study, it has become closely associated with dogmatic quantitative science and

---

37. Stephen Bales, "Academic Library as Crypto-Temple," *Class and Librarianship: Essays at the Intersection of Information, Labor and Capital*, eds. Erik Estep and Nathaniel Enright (Sacramento, CA: Library Juice Press, forthcoming, 2015).

the scientific method in particular. This ideological hijacking and transformation of science into Science has spread out from the hard sciences, manifesting in the social sciences with the legacy of positivism initiated by Comte. According to Scruton, scientism is also beginning to infiltrate the humanities with the creation of fields of study like neuroaesthetics,[38] and disciplines that use "scientific forms and categories in order to give the appearance of science to unscientific ways of thinking."[39]

Academic librarians, especially those practicing in the U.S. where materialist positivism maintains a strong ideological grip on the academy, seem to by default, and in a way that is in keeping with the prevailing trends in neoliberal capitalist societies, perceive reality as both linear and metaphysically discrete. That is, effects are seen as following from determinative causes, and it is often the goal of contemporary LIS research endeavors to make clear distinctions between causes and effects. In the process, individual phenomena are reduced to discrete particulars and largely considered as ontologically noncontiguous, resulting many times in a Cartesian differentiation between matter and ideas. LIS graduate students, for instance, all learn about the physical and cognitive paradigms as the two major and counterpoised theoretical paradigms in LIS research. That such an approach is seen frequently in academic settings, and hence the MCALs, should not be particularly surprising considering that the use-value of the library itself is quite often portrayed as an autonomous tool that is employed by people as means to various ends. For example, the MCAL is seen as a means towards obtaining an education and as an apparatus for methodically creating and disseminating new knowledge. As a result of the noncontiguous consideration of persons and places, the role of people and ideas as an organic component of the MCAL may be undervalued.

Compounding the historically entrenched, deeply sublimated, and pro-status quo ideologies found in the MCAL *qua* modern capitalist

---

38. Roger Scruton, "Scientism in the Arts and Humanities," *The New Atlantis* 40 (Fall 2013), 36.

39. Ibid., 46.

institution, is the powerful grip that traditional scientific approaches have over LIS, as evidenced by the dominant role of empirical science in the LIS research literature;[40] empirical Science has become a primary pedagogical model for training new library professionals. This ideological orientation is not surprising, considering the role of the late-nineteenth and early-twentieth century documentation movement in the development of LIS that coincided with the rapid technological advances made during the second half of the twentieth century. The LIS literature offers study after study that reduce complex social phenomena to sets of numbers stripped of qualitative content and the meaningful consideration of possible overdetermining factors related to sociocultural milieu. As with idealism, non-dialectical materialism results in its fair share of simplistic abstractions.

Take, for example, recent research efforts dealing with library anxiety, a state-based anxiety that manifests itself in aversive behaviors on the part of the library user concerning library staff and library resources. The majority of research reports concerning library anxiety are empirical, quantitative studies, with the remainder being empirical, qualitative studies. To my knowledge there are currently no critical/cultural research reports available concerning library anxiety. Instead, the available research typically reduces the phenomena to the interaction of two entities, the library and the user. It seeks to find a correlational link between the library and the user, and then it generalizes these conclusions to large but simplistically abstract categories such as First Year Students, Graduate Students, ESL Students, or Distance Students. Correlations are often made between abstract categories such as between library users and abstract dimensions such as "Barriers with Staff," "Comfort with the Library," and "Mechanical Barriers,"[41] often at the expense of much

---

40. Karen E. Pettigrew and Lynne McKechnie, "The Use of Theory in Information Science Research," *Journal of the American Society for Information Science and Technology* 52, no. 1 (2001): 66.

41. Sharon Bostick, "The Development and Validation of the Library Anxiety Scale," (PhD dissertation, Wayne State University, 1992).

meaningful content. For example, in a study of perfectionism and library anxiety among graduate students, Jiao and Onwuegbuzie, found that

> Specifically, graduate students with relatively high levels of socially prescribed perfectionism tend to have higher levels of library anxiety associated with "affective barriers," "comfort with the library," and "mechanical barriers." These findings provide partial support for the overall hypothesis that library anxiety is related to perfectionism.[42]

This finding, that perfectionism is related in some way to library anxiety, is certainly valuable information. Indeed, the authors are correct in noting that their findings provide "partial support" to the argument that library anxiety correlates to perfectionism. The partial nature of empirical findings, however, is endemic to non-dialectical materialism. Implemented in support of a dialectical approach, the findings may be of more value. As part of a body of research based on a metaphysical materialist worldview, the study becomes one more element of a collection of partialities, assorted bricks in a half-sighted science. The non-dialectical materialist, however, often fails to see, or even look for, the complete picture.

These sorts of non-dialectical materialist approaches are part and parcel of the training that librarians receive in their graduate educations if, in fact they receive any formal training in research methods. Analyzing the types of research methodologies used in LIS doctoral dissertations, Powell found that only 1.9 percent of dissertations between 1925 and 1972, and only 1.4 percent between 1973 and 1981 could be classified as "theoretical" approaches, while a stunning 44.2 percent and 56.1 percent for these respective years relied on survey methodology.[43]

---

42. Qun G. Jiao and Anthony J. Onwuegbuzie, "Perfectionism and Library Anxiety among Graduate Students," *Journal of Academic Librarianship* 25, no. 5 (1998): 368.

43. Ronald R. Powell, "Research Competence for Ph.D. Students in Library and Information Science," *Journal of Education for Library and Information Science* 36, no. 4 (Fall 1995): 324.

Therefore, non-dialectical materialism, like non-dialectical objective idealism, ignores both historical context and the interlacing nature of everything that exists in the past, the present, and between things past and present. The majority of work on library anxiety, for example, considers its objects of analysis as things, attributes, and relationships, with little regard for these objects' becoming, changing, and passing out of existence. These objects of analysis, while being physically material or arising from material interactions or substances, such as the assertion that thought processes and identity arise from the physical matter of the human brain, are turned into inviolate realities. That is, the objects of study are ontologically separated from one another and hence definable outside of their relationships to other entities. Again, as with non-dialectical objective idealism, when such a worldview becomes entrenched by the dominant class it essentially becomes myth and tradition, stifling analysis and critique.

Both the scholarly research coming out of American research entities (particularly the professional library school programs and academic research libraries), as well as the output of mainstream American popular publications, are typically presented using "traditional" scientific methods, metaphysical theoretical assumptions, and/or idealist philosophies. Although many of these publications have provided us with important perspectives and conclusions concerning libraries and librarianship—they arguably have done much to make academic libraries into what they are today—employing these intellectual frameworks remains, nevertheless, partial and one-sided. That is, the discoveries made using such hegemonically sanctioned ontologies and research procedures have often failed to adequately account for the multiplicity of social phenomena and the interaction between these phenomena when looking at the MCAL as an analyzable unit for understanding the existing social formation, be these phenomena physical, mental, or historical.

In a letter to the French Marxist Inessa Armand, Lenin wrote that the "whole spirit of Marxism, its whole system, demands that each proposition should be considered only historically, only in connection with others, only in the concrete experience of history."[44] Any intellectually honest critical analyst must recognize the sterility inherent in applying traditional "laboratory control" concepts to social research. Context is key, and context may only be understood clearly when considered both synchronically (in the moment, in the ahistorical now) and diachronically (across time, historically).

As an alternative means of critiquing and understanding society, dialectical materialism allows researchers to move beyond the dualistic conceptions of reality that have remained a major part of the human psyche for millennia. That is, dialectical materialism does much to mend the artificial separation of physical objects and human mind that has for centuries plagued humans' discernment of, and approach to, reality.

A Third Way: Dialectical Materialism as an Alternative

Non-dialectical objective idealism often conflicts with its chief rival, non-dialectical materialism. But objective idealism also coexists with non-dialectical materialism in an uneasy truce. Today's ideological waters are, in fact, particularly cloudy, with idealisms sometimes being held by many people, including members of the scientific community, simultaneously with the basic tenets of non-dialectical materialism.[45] But those people who have worked in a library may sense intuitively that there is more to where they work and what they do than such non-dialectical approaches can address adequately.

In the companion book to his 1980 television documentary series *Cosmos*, Carl Sagan celebrated the library's immense scale in terms of the depth and breadth of its intellectual cache and the continually unfolding nature of the knowledge which it incubates, cultivates, and distributes.

---

44. V.I. Lenin, "Letter to Inessa Armand," in *Lenin Collected Works*, vol. 35, trans. Andrew Rothstein (Moscow: Progress Publishers, 1976), 250.

45. Elaine Howard Ecklund and Christopher P. Scheitle, "Religion among Academic Scientists: Distinctions, Disciplines, and Demographics," *Social Problems* 54, no. 2 (May 2007): 297, found that 48 percent of U.S. scientists and social scientists consider themselves to have a religious affiliation.

He wrote that the "great libraries of the world contain millions of volumes, the equivalent of 10^{14} bits of information in words, and perhaps 10^{15} bits in pictures. This is ten thousand times more information than in our genes, and about ten times more than in our brains."[46] Today, just a few decades after Sagan wrote this, the scale of the library has grown exponentially, thanks largely to ceaseless innovation in information technology, telecommunications, and digitization processes.[47] The volume of electronically available information resources has increased dramatically since 1980, and the computer systems developed to access these resources have increased greatly in both sophistication and efficacy. The breakneck pace of the information revolution is largely a consequence of technology's intimate connection with the research and education endeavors of which academic libraries are organic components. But such codeterminations also involve things that are not typically as closely associated with the academic library as information technology. Advances in disparate (but themselves related) areas like the health sciences, civil engineering, sociology, human rights, and popular culture all participate in intricate feedback loops that are associated with academic libraries in various degrees of relationship; but they are, nonetheless, all associated. These relationships are myriad, tendrillar, and interwoven. They include processes seen as existing outside of the library's traditional domain that ultimately extend throughout the spheres of culture and politics in a comprehensive overdetermination of social reality. The academic library is by no means unique in its possession of a relational, dialectical constitution. A dialectical understanding of nature demands that one consider all phenomena, all of reality in fact, as intrinsically dialectical. What the academic library is, however, is an immensely (if quietly) powerful institution. And, if we consider the

---

46. Carl Sagan, *Cosmos*, 1st ed. (New York: Random House, 1980), 281.

47. LiLi Li, in *Emerging Technologies for Academic Libraries in the Digital Age* (Oxford, UK: Chandos Publishing, 2009), 15, wrote that a Google search (complete science fiction in 1980) for "emerging technologies" generated 12,300,000 search results. In 2014, he same search by the present author yielded 21,500,000 results.

academic library as an organic facet of the society in which it operates, we have an important vantage point for observing both the institution and the society.

The ancient Greek philosopher Heraclitus (fl. sixth century BCE) developed a philosophy of cosmos in constant motion, and his ideas are of particular importance to the history and development of dialectics. Heraclitus likened reality to flowing water, providing a foundational trope for an understanding of reality as flux. "The river where you set your foot just now is gone," said the Ephesian philosopher, "those waters giving way to constant change."[48] Meditation on the MCAL suggests that the complexity and interconnectedness of the institution possesses a diachronic temporal aspect in addition to a spatial extension that encompasses the multitudinous objects and phenomena that coexist in the now. The MCAL is forever in the act of becoming something new, of reworking itself through the interplay of relationships that comprise it and that connect it, either directly or indirectly, to the greater social reality.

Even if we tentatively agree that that the MCAL, as well as everything else that exists as real (i.e., material), is characterized by complexity, interconnection, and change, difficulties arise because of humanity's tendency to "fix" reality (librarians appear to be particularly fond of doing this). As noted in the preceding discussions of non-dialectical objective idealism and non-dialectical materialism, people want to impose permanence upon flux, to circumscribe the reality with which they interact, to tame it. In a way, establishing clear ontological boundaries makes our reality more palatable. The universe becomes more cognizable when we cement its phenomena by naming them and defining them. But even though structuring reality is necessary for us to successfully navigate our lives, we risk undervaluing the processes of being that are equally important for understanding the phenomenal world.

---

48. Heraclitus, *Fragments: The Collected Wisdom of Heraclitus*, trans. Brooks Haxton (New York: Viking, 2001), 27.

It only requires a small bit of additional brainwork to move from this realization, that all things are in constant transition, to the realization that one should maintain a healthy skepticism towards all things deemed static or inviolate, whether that status as incorruptible has been gained through uncritical faith in the scientific method, expert opinion, common sense, religion, or some combination of these things. This cognitive movement is consistent with our observation of reality as characterized by change, that is, as dialectical. We change ourselves and our reality through the process of mentally accounting for our unfolding existence.

The dialectic of academic librarianship is nothing more than the application of this reflective and active approach towards reality qua flux to the academic library as a social institution and academic librarianship as an aspect of this institution's being and identity. It aims for the critical apperception of the academic library as an integral locus and expression of the constantly changing total reality. The dialectician sees the academic library as a historical material locus of human action that is at once profoundly generative of social reality and profoundly conservative of power structures within this same social reality. This major contradiction, transformation and stasis, is a source of tension within the library, and academic librarians are often conflicted as to their roles in an institution that serves as both a forge of the new and a coercive tool of the dominant culture.

The Physical and Mental Presence of the MCAL

I wrote above that the technological developments going on within and through the MCAL involve not only physical components like information technology, but also ideas. Most everyone agrees that the academic library consists not only of physical environs and collections, but also of the people who study and work there. But what about the actual thinking produced in the library, or the ideas that are produced about the MCAL itself? Do these cognitive and apparently ephemeral things also contribute to the library's composition? The conclusion seems obvious: to know physical reality, one must factor in cognition and its related phenomena and consequences.

If the MCAL is comprised of thought and ideas as well as physical matter, the way to understand the MCAL *in toto*, or at least as fully as is as pragmatic for an effective analysis, is to examine how these apparently dissimilar components work together. The materialist dialectics that I expound upon in the remaining chapters holds that all things interact with each other to realize the total reality as the objective whole. Everything has a material effect on each other as well as the total reality, regardless of their individual substantiality, and hence they are all, regardless of physicality, materially present. Acknowledging the material presence of the MCAL as both a product and producer of human history sensitizes the critical analyst to patterns of change. It allows analysts to define the ways in which historical moments are unique while they are, at the same time, contingent on the material realities of the past. At the same time that the careful consideration of history sharpens our understanding of our social being as a movement that unfurls not wholly chaotically, but with some sort of conditionality and predictability, it draws our attention to similarities and patterns in social structures that extend across time. It punctures the validity of those elements deemed unchangeable and eternal in nature when, in actuality, only the total reality is eternal. Therefore, to understand where we are heading, we must understand where we are located in the present by way of the past. If the MCAL is the object of our analysis, how and why is it materially present to us here and now? Where are we located in Heraclitus' river, the constantly moving torrent of change that, as Sagan suggested, is currently gushing forth at a remarkable clip? What does viewing the MCAL in context mean within a theory of impermanency?

Chapter 1 introduced the importance of context to the analysis of the MCAL. That is, critical analysts should understand the past and present in order to effectively conceive possible futures and work towards positive outcomes. I presented the neoliberal capitalist social formation as the dominant system that structures modern society, and as a system embodied and realized within the current MCAL. The best way to escape the interminable task of pinning down libraries and librarianship is to acknowledge, once and for all, that libraries and librarianship can never be pinned down. The most effective way to view the MCAL in light of this conclusion lies with the third way listed at the start of the present chapter, to approach ultimate reality as "the material interaction of both mental concepts and physical objects as they mesh in human culture and history as material presence." Although it may not seem intuitive at first, and librarians are not trained in LIS schools to think and act like this, approaching the academic library in a dialectical fashion provides the academic library practitioner with some theoretical flexibility, clear vision (both historically and in terms of the future), and the ability to both see and affect a positive potentiality in terms of change.

Dialectical materialism is a philosophy and method that works as an integrative and monistic alternative to views of the cosmos that apply artificial metaphysical conditions to reality. It allows researchers and practitioners, and preferably, researchers as practitioners, to understand and critique the academic library as a historically placed element of the materialized matter/mind confluence. It allows theoretically informed academic librarians to discern the academic library as both materialized human knowledge and the nexus of a materially and theoretically present locus that reflects, responds to, and helps to drive modern neoliberal capitalist society. This philosophical approach provides us with a way to see beyond the received views of the MCAL as a more-or-less static set of ideas, or as a static set of physical things.

Chapter 3

DIALECTICAL MATERIAL MONISM AS A VEHICLE FOR UNDERSTANDING THE MCAL IN FLUX

The previous chapter offered two views of the academic library that are realized as either conscious systematic approaches or as a broadly construed worldview (or possibly sometimes both of these things at once): non-dialectical objective idealism and non-dialectical materialism. Both of these philosophical approaches were deemed lacking in that they do not adequately account for change, and in that they do not fully account for the complexity inherent in reality as a totality. That is, by privileging either mind or physical matter over its ontological counterpart, one tends to be left with a partially conceived reality. Neither of these two ways, as a result, lends itself particularly well to the sort of active professional practice that encourages and effects progressive societal transformation. Instead, they validate the status quo, either through devaluing the importance of physical reality or by ignoring the potential of mind by reducing it to the mechanical action of neural physiology. How then does adopting a dialectical materialist view of reality allow us to better understand the academic library and change it?

The critical/cultural study of libraries and librarianship remains on the periphery of LIS. Dialectical materialism is a tricky subject of discussion for several reasons. First and foremost, it is smeared because of its association with communist ideologies and politics. This reticence towards dialectical materialism is felt in academia because of an often uninformed fear of this controversial history of political application, its anti-establishment standpoints, and the present domination of neoliberal ideology. The legacy of Stalinism and much of the twentieth-century Soviet scholarship has resulted in official strains of Soviet dialectical materialism (DIAMAT) that hijacked the philosophy and transformed it into something akin to a state religion, an ideology that is overly dogmatic, schematic, and prescriptive. This dilapidation of theory is a historical development that Marx would have found to be profoundly disturbing. Dialectical materialism has never been perceived as a culturally intuitive philosophy in the United States, and those people who actively espouse it have been routinely relegated to the position of "other" in American society. This outsider status is also reinforced in the oftentimes low priority given to critical approaches by American LIS graduate level training programs, as well as the MCAL's bureaucratic tendencies which discourage critical introspection and reflexivity in favor of keeping the MCAL and other entities, e.g., the system of higher education in the wider sense, up and running as they are.

Dialectical materialism, also referred to as materialist dialectics (the two terms are used interchangeably here), means constant transformation. This transformation is the basis of human social reality, in a material sense, and change as a means for arriving at an intellectual understanding and modification of this material reality. Dialectics is a conversation. It is a natural movement that effects a transformation through an encounter and the resolution of a material conflict through a material synthesis: the famous thesis, antithesis, synthesis formula. Things constantly encounter other things, and they change as a result of this interaction. Although this idea may not seem profound when taken at face value, it becomes more so when it is considered as a principle for understanding and engaging with reality. That is, materialist dialectic as an organizing schema allows a knower to account for the phenomena of emergent reality (I use the term phenomena broadly to represent physical objects in the singular and collective sense, physical and mental processes, ideas, and relations between objects) in a manner that reaches beyond traditional explicitly or implicitly held positivist notions of cause and effect, incorporating consideration of change, relationships, and totality. Understanding how materialist dialectics works means understanding how all things matter; the philosophy vigorously refutes the Great Man theory.

As I present it here, the dialectic of academic librarianship is an ontological, epistemological, and practical application of a mode of thought and understanding of reality to the historical and material reality of the MCAL. It accepts the institution as constantly changing both in terms of space and time. The MCAL sits at the nexus of a multitude of ideas, processes, and physical realities. It is woven into neoliberal capitalist society and serves as a historically-situated sociocultural anchor and ideological engine that also contains the germ of social change. The MCAL's constituencies, including both the possessing and the dispossessed, and its functionaries, including both the library's staff and faculty, also interact dialectically with the institution. Having argued that non-dialectical approaches to reality lack the historical perspective necessary for change, this chapter now presents dialectical material monism as an alternative approach. First, I briefly review the history of dialectics and materialism in primarily Western society. Following this, I outline the basic tenets of materialist dialectics to set the stage for their application to the MCAL. I then focus on one particular reading of materialist dialectics, dialectical material monism, and propose that the ideas of the mid-nineteenth century philosopher Joseph Dietzgen work as an effective method for achieving a critical understanding of how the MCAL integrates and interacts with its late capitalist milieu.

A Brief History of Dialectics, Materialism, and Dialectical Materialism

As seen with the introduction to Heraclitus in the previous chapter, dialectical explanations for reality are nothing new. Materialist accounts of reality have likewise endured for millennia and across multiple cultures. These two concepts, dialectics and materialism, have long acted as legitimate intellectual counter-positions to, respectively, formal logic and theoretical idealism. The fortunes of both dialectics and materialism have shifted back and forth over the centuries, often due to religious and political factors. Both concepts peaked in the ancient Greco-Roman world, converged in the mid-nineteenth and early-twentieth centuries in the works of Marx and his followers, and then this convergence fell out of favor in the second half of the twentieth century, largely as a result of the Cold War and the subsequent failure of the Soviet Union and various other communist regimes. Regardless of communism's poor political fortunes, materialist dialectics has remained an undercurrent in both politics and academia. Marxist thought and dialectics continues to inform critical approaches to research, including feminist theory, queer theory, post-colonial theory, and British cultural studies. Furthermore, recent world events, such as the increasing globalization of markets in the 1990s and the world financial crisis of the 2000s, have rekindled interest in Marxist analyses. This resurgence of dialectical materialism is not particularly surprising. The philosophy has long provided a means for understanding social change. In his book *First as Tragedy, Then as Farce*, Žižek wrote that "in the ongoing confusion, there is certainly sufficient material to cause us to think things through."[1] Combined with materialism, dialectics becomes a practicable method for doing just this: for understanding recurring crises in the economy and culture, as well as implementing changes to these things.

As a philosophical position, dialectics can be traced back to two ancient thinkers, Lao-Tzu (fl. sixth century BCE) in the East and Heraclitus in the West. The writings of these two men are sufficiently similar to one another that their independent developments reinforce the notion that dialectical thinking stretches across cultural and geographical boundaries. Lao-Tze, the originator of the Daoist philosophy, conceived of reality as existing in perpetual motion and characterized by relational interdependence and contradictions:

> Being and beingless generate each other;
> Difficult and easy form each other;
> Long and short shape each other;

---

1. Slavoj Žižek, *First as Tragedy, Then as Farce* (London: Verso, 2009), 11.

Note and voice match each other.
(Such are all perennial.)[2]

The philosophical edifice that has been constructed around Lao-Tze's ideas is an example of dialectical monism, the folding of subjective multiplicity into the objective total reality.

Similarly to Lao-Tze, Heraclitus developed his own philosophy of change. We have already seen that he likened reality to flowing water, providing a foundational metaphor for reality as flux. He also wrote that this constant change resulted in the emergence of the new from the old: "By cosmic rule, as day yields night, so winter summer, war peace, plenty, famine. All things change. Fire penetrates the lump of myrrh, until the joining bodies die and rise again in smoke called incense."[3] Heraclitus's thought prefigured other, now well-known concepts of modern dialectic—such as the interpenetration of opposites and the existence and clash of contradictions— with cryptic verse like "the sea is both pure and tainted, healthy and good haven to the fish, to men impotable and deadly."[4] Although only fragments of the philosopher's works have survived, the longevity of his ideas demonstrates the tenacious hold that dialectics have on the human mind.

Even though Heraclitus embraced both a dialectical outlook and a proto-materialist outlook, for he believed that everything is composed of—somewhat confusingly, considering the enduring fame of his river metaphor—fire, the two concepts were by no means definitively linked until the nineteenth century. Materialism maintained its presence throughout the history of ancient philosophy, with its primary exponents including the atomists Leucippus (fl. mid-fifth century BCE) and Democritus (born ca. 460-57 BCE). Plato (lived 429-347 BCE), however, subordinated physical reality to idealism. He incorporated dialectics

---

2. Lao-Tse, *Dao De Jing*, trans. Edmund Ryden (Oxford, UK: Oxford University Press, 2008), 7.

3. Heraclitus, *Fragments: The Collected Wisdom of Heraclitus*, trans. Brooks Haxton (New York: Viking, 2001), 25.

4. Ibid., 35.

as a method to refine concepts in order to achieve knowledge of the ideal forms, and his philosophy later became entangled with Christian religious thought, further mystifying the latter. Aristotle (lived 384-322 BCE), actually more of a moderate realist than a pure idealist, championed dialectics as a means for obtaining insight into the arche, or the basic axioms of a science. After such arche had been identified, the Aristotelian scientist could then construct syllogisms in order to define reality in terms of essence. Aristotle's influence was so enormous that his philosophy became something akin to holy writ in the Middle Ages and up to the development of modern science. Despite the decline of Platonism and Aristotelianism as dominant worldviews, both of these philosophers' views continue to influence modern thinkers.

Hegel modernized dialectics, seeing history as the unfolding of the Ultimate Idea or World Spirit. He saw this process as the relentless resolution of contradictions which coexist and conflict in reality, and he spent his career examining and systematizing this movement through history. Difficult works like the *Science of Logic* set forth the dialectical principles by which ideas come into conflict and are continually refined, relegating formal logic to a support role. His dialectics embodied a strange dichotomy, a fire and crucible explanation for reality that, at the same time, conservatively positioned the Prussian state at the pinnacle of Western civilization. Not surprisingly, these contradictory positions led to a division among Hegel's followers, with one faction embracing the revolutionary nature of his dialectics in order to develop their own radical left philosophies, and the other faction embracing a reactionary conservatism.

Marx initiated a transformation of Hegel's dialectics, synthesizing it with the materialist ideas of Ludwig Feuerbach. Marx and Engels were among those New Hegelians who adopted far left political positions and saw the power of Hegel's dialectical categories as an explanation for and means of radical social change; a change that, if consciously organized, would benefit humanity through resolving the glaring contradictions found in modern social relations. The key contradiction for Marx was the conflict between labor and capital. Marx saw Hegelian dialectics as, "the basic form of all dialectics, but only after it has been stripped of its mystical form,"[5] that is, as effective only after it had been removed from the realm of ideas. He inverted Hegel's philosophy, shedding idealism and providing dialectics with a materialist basis inspired by Feuerbach. Marx wrote that

> The mystification which dialectic suffers in Hegel's hands by no means prevents him from being the first to present its general forms of motion in a comprehensive and conscious manner. With him it is standing on its head. It must be inverted, in order to discover the rational kernel within the mystical shell.[6]

Marx concluded that change worked itself out materially through time, in space, and by means of the clash and conjunction of historically situated material practices and phenomena. This philosophical inversion provided social critics with explanatory power for understanding and critiquing historical events and the capitalist social formation. Furthermore, putting Hegel on his feet provided a practical way forward by identifying a transformative praxis that combined concrete action, theoretical understanding, and progressive change. If one defines what exists to be a ceaselessly changing material reality, effective theory may also be conceived as a shifting and non-dogmatic material force that takes part in the realization of this material reality. In fact, because human cognition becomes a function of matter under this philosophy, it is subject to the same dialectical motions as all other objects and phenomena. Marx and Engels concluded that, because of the nature of reality, and thus because of the material constitution and material effect of theory, man "must prove the truth, i.e., the reality and power, the this-worldliness of his thinking in practice. The dispute over the reality or non-reality of thinking which is isolated from practice is a

---

5. Karl Marx, "Marx to Kugelmann in Hanover, 6 March 1868," Marxists.org, accessed July 14, 2014, https://www.marxists.org/archive/marx/works/1868/letters/68_03_06-abs.htm.

6. Karl Marx, *Capital: A Critique of the Political Economy*, vol. I., trans. Ben Fowkes (London: Penguin Books, 1976), 103.

purely scholastic question."[7] That is, theory is human practice in that, if theory is to be considered anything more than a solipsistic mental exercise or pseudo-religion, it must extend beyond cognition in order to test and transform the objects of its analysis, as well as transmogrify cognition, physical reality, theory itself. This conclusion means that if the critical analyst understands the basic propositions of dialectics and attunes herself to dialectical thinking, she can effectively become consonant with the object of her analysis and positively impact reality, theory, and her own cognitive and physical existence in the process. The goal of philosophy, Marx wrote in his eleventh "Theses on Feuerbach," is to change the world.[8]

Materialist dialectics permeates Marx's writings and his penetrating dialectical approach to analyses shines through in such works as The *Communist Manifesto* and the three volumes of *Capital*, his magnum opus. Marx, however, died without leaving any thorough written explanation of his theory and method, leaving to Engels the task of explicating dialectical materialism. Engels's primary exposition of materialist dialectics is found in his *Anti-Dühring*, where he sets forth the basic principles for Marx and his dialectics. The book is a tedious and often impenetrable polemic against the theories of the socialist but anti-Marxist philosopher Eugene Dühring. It sets forth Engels's interpretations of Hegelian dialectical motion in terms of its impact on the material world, historical development, and the capitalist mode of production. In his later years, Engels continued to explore materialist dialectics in texts like *The Dialectics of Nature*, which applies dialectical materialism to explain the gamut of phenomena found in the natural world. Engels was greatly responsible for the formal codification of materialist dialectics and method. His work arguably served as the foundation for the Marxist-Leninist theory of the twentieth century, which may be accused of sticking over-dogmatically to many of Engels's formulations. Such provincialism,

---

7. Karl Marx, "Theses on Feuerbach," in *The German Ideology* (Amherst, NY: Prometheus Books, 1998), 569.

8. Ibid., 571.

however, runs counter to the spirit of dialectical materialism. Because of its scope and flexibility, Marx and Engels's innovative approach is unlimited in terms of its application to the study of social phenomena, and researchers have used Marxist concepts to parse topics in political science, economics, history, sociology, psychology, anthropology, and popular culture. The two men gave critical analysts the necessary tools to study and transform socio-cultural institutions like the MCAL.

Although Lenin is many times rightly condemned for the excesses of the early years of the Soviet Union, as well as for prefiguring the subsequent horrors of Stalinism, he further established materialist dialectics as a revolutionary philosophical system and developed theories of praxis. However, the rigidity of what Marxism-Leninism would become, particularly under the Stalinist regime's development of a deterministic, dogmatic party-line, and ultimately conservative dialectical materialism, aka DIAMAT, resulted in Soviet philosophy's languishment. This right wing communism, however, would spark progressive, left-wing Marxist attempts at salvaging materialist dialectics. This pushback against Soviet dogma attempted to rescue dialectic from being reduced to rigid unequivocal Truths, the very things that Marxists like to polemicize against. Karl Korsch and Anton Pannekoek are regarded as two of the founders of the "Western Marxism," that flourished in France and at the Frankfurt Institute of Social Research (the "Frankfurt School"). The Western Marxists took aim at DIAMAT and many sought to reestablish dialectical practice with its Hegelian and Marxist origins. Henri Lefebvre is among the best known Western materialist dialecticians. Like Korsch and Pannekoek, Lefebvre was ferociously anti-Stalinist and worked hard to save dialectics from its Stalinist vulgarization. He published profusely on dialectics and the reproduction of social relations in such texts as *The Production of Space* and *The Critique of Everyday Life*. Jean-Paul Sartre also raised the profile of dialectics in the mid-twentieth century by defending Marxism in his *Critique of Dialectical Reasoning*, where he attempted to square dialectics with existentialism and explored praxis in relationship to human freedom. Following Stalin's death in 1953 and his subsequent repudiation by Khrushchev, new vistas opened up in terms of academic inquiry in the Soviet bloc countries. Evald Ilyenkov, for instance, approached Lenin's work on dialectics with fresh eyes and wrote largely unfettered by the dogmatism of the recent past. Like the Western Marxists, he worked to reconnect materialist dialectics with its roots and to save it from bureaucracy.

Possibly the most visible contemporary proponent of materialist dialectics is Bertell Ollman, who helped revive materialist dialectics following the heyday of structuralism in the 1960s and 1970s and the gains made by neoliberal capitalism in the 1980s and 1990s. Ollman resuscitated dialectical materialism as an accessible means for critical inquiry with texts like *Dance of the Dialectic* and *Dialectical Investigations*, books that clearly describe dialectical logic and practice and are a relief to anyone drowning in Hegel's obfuscations and Marx's drier works. These renovations have proven to be timely. The first years of the twenty-first century have seen major clashes between competing ideologies (e.g., Western market economies and radical Islamist movements), dynamic progress and reaction in terms of basic human rights (e.g., the escalating struggle for LGBT rights), and the near collapse of the capitalist world economy with the great recession of 2009. Modern dialectics, although left for dead during the last half of the twentieth century through conservative pronouncements like Fukuyama's[9] *End of History*, is a dynamic worldview that, through refining itself by means of conflict and synthesis, is proving itself once again to be a valuable tool for analyzing today's socio-political and ideological environments.

Dialectical Materialism as a Method of Social Critique

As I use the term in this book, dialectical materialism is a confrontation of material realities resulting in new material realities. Dialectical motion is always reciprocal, mutually conditioning, transformative, and responsive, affecting all of the parties to any encounter. There is no

---

9. Francis Fukuyama, *The End of History and the Last Man* (New York: The Free Press, 1992).

reason why there should be only two parties involved, although limiting to two phenomena often allows for ease of description and a starting point for analysis. Dialectical materialism is not a primitive or vulgar metaphysical materialism that reduces thought and mind to atoms.

What is generally undisputed among dialectical materialists is that they espouse a philosophy that fundamentally incorporates history into an understanding of reality and necessitates a material practice as a means for effectively actualizing material change. These two aspects are mutually conditioning. That is, to consciously examine and understand reality is to engage in materially realized action that accompanies a material transformation in both the subject (she who cognizes and acts) and the object (parts of the wider reality of which she who cognizes and acts is engaged with in a relational trajectory). The fruit of this creative conversation is the material transformation enacted through the critical analyst's act of critique. The critical analyst transforms reality by identifying major contradictions found in its phenomena, divining how these contradictions affect the phenomena in question and related phenomena, confronting these contradictions, and working both mentally and physically towards their resolution. As a prism, the dialectical materialist approach allows the critical analyst to see the MCAL as part and whole at one and the same time, and as a result, to better understand the role of the library and its material presence in today's society. The positive outcome of such diagnoses is strategically derived prescriptive action.

But that which constitutes the material basis of reality has long been a contested issue among dialectical materialists. This argument may be divided into two primary positions: the claim that the development of material reality through history is determined by economic forces (the base) and the claim that the sociocultural and ideological forces (the superstructure) possess a certain amount of autonomy, which also determines the development of material reality and may even affect the economic base and forces of production. The former position, what Cohen named the "primacy thesis,"[10] has traditionally represented

---

10. G.A. Cohen, *Karl Marx's Theory of History: A Defence*, expanded ed.

the view of the Marxist orthodoxy, and, according to Sayer[11] may be traced back to a famous passage from Marx's preface to his *Critique of Political Economy*:

> In the social production of their existence, men inevitably enter into definite relations, which are independent of their will, namely relations of production appropriate to a given stage in the development of their material forces of production. The totality of these relations of production constitutes the economic structure of society, the real foundation, on which arises a legal and political superstructure and to which correspond definite forms of social consciousness. The mode of production of material life conditions the general process of social, political and intellectual life. It is not the consciousness of men that determines their existence, but their social existence that determines their consciousness.[12]

Sayer noted that challenges arise to the primacy thesis's interpretation of the base/superstructure divide when one takes into account the later writings of Marx and Engels, and particularly Engels's personal correspondence.[13] Although Engels was by no means consistent on the issue of the historical determination of reality, the letters that he wrote in his later life, particularly an 1890 letter to Bloch, bemoan the tendencies towards economic determinism then prevalent in Marxist circles. Sayer noted that in this letter, Engels wrote that the economic factor was not the only determining one, but only "finally asserts itself" in the final instance.[14] That is,

> The economic situation is the basis, but the various components of the superstructure—political forms of the class struggle and its consequences, such as: constitutions drawn up by the victorious class after a

---

(Princeton, NJ: Princeton University Press, 2001), 134.

11. Derek Sayer, *The Violence of Abstraction: The Analytic Foundations of Historical Materialism* (Oxford, UK: Basil Blackwell, 1987), 1.

12. Karl Marx, *A Contribution to the Critique of Political Economy*, ed. Maurice Dobb, trans. S.W. Ryazanskaya (New York: International Publishers, 1970), 20-21.

13. Sayer, *Violence of Abstraction*, 5-9.

14. Ibid.

successful battle, etc., juridical forms and *even the reflections of all these actual struggles in the minds of the participants, political, juristic, philosophical theories, religious views and their further development into systems of dogmas* [emphasis added by present author]—also exercise their influence upon the course of the historical struggles and in many cases determine their *form* in particular.[15]

Of particular interest to my monistic understanding of dialectical materialism is the portion of this quote where Engels refers to *systems of dogmas* as working to determine material reality.

The dialectical materialism that I adopt and advocate herein for applying to LIS theory and practice was espoused by the mid-nineteenth century Marxist philosopher Joseph Dietzgen. Dietzgen was a laborer, a tanner by trade. He was also an autodidact and a contemporary and admirer of Marx and Engels. Remarkably, Dietzgen developed his own version of dialectical materialism independently of those two scholars, in the process earning their praise; Marx even introduced him as "our philosopher" at the Fifth Congress of the International Working Men's Association.[16] His philosophy is now relatively unknown, although it is finding renewed exposure through the works of current dialecticians like Ollman. This obscurity is possibly due to the ascendance of orthodox Marxism-Leninism in the twentieth century.[17] Nonetheless, Dietzgen's development of dialectical materialism, described by his son Eugene as "cosmic-monistic philosophy,"[18] complemented the early humanistic work of Marx and was championed by the left-wing council communist Pannekoek in opposition to the orthodox Marxism of the time.[19] Burns

---

15. Karl Marx and Friedrich Engels, *Selected Correspondence 1846-1889 with Commentary and Notes*, trans. Dona Torr (London: Lawrence & Wishart, 1936), 475.

16. Eugene Dietzgen, "Joseph Dietzgen: A Sketch of His Life," in Joseph Dietzgen, *Some of the Philosophical Essays on Socialism and Science, Religion, Ethics, Critique-of-Reason and the World-at-Large*, eds. Eugene Dietzgen and Joseph Dietzgen, Jr., trans. M. Berr and T. Rothstein (Chicago, IL: Charles H. Kerr, 1917), 15.

17. Adam Buick, "Joseph Dietzgen," *Radical Philosophy* 10 (1975): 6.

18. Dietzgen, "Joseph Dietzgen: A Sketch of His Life," 13.

19. Tony Burns, "Joseph Dietzgen and the History of Marxism," *Science &*

claimed that Dietzgen's philosophy does not present anything particularly novel concerning dialectical materialism, even if it was developed apart from Marx and Engels.[20] But I believe that Dietzgen offered a valuable ontological and epistemological approach to dialectical materialism that takes reality fully into consideration. His is an account of reality that acknowledges the prior nature of matter over mind, i.e., that the mind would not exist without matter, but then refuses to subordinate the latter to the former in terms of the material reality of its consequences on society and social classes. In this way, Dietzgen transforms Spinozist philosophy into radical social theory. His theories are excellent tools for confronting the oftentimes rigid sociocultural and bureaucratic structures ingrained in the MCAL and academic librarianship.

Dietzgen's dialectical materialism is a neutral monism as opposed to the strict materialism championed by orthodox Marxists. The philosophy is expansive and flexible, and may even be described as spiritual in a Spinozist sense. The key idea behind this conception of reality is that the universe is an objective, unified totality that is at the same time comprised of an infinite number of forever changing subjective phenomena; i.e., that everything that exists, be it physical or mental, may be said to be equally a part of this one universal whole and, therefore, as equally "real":

> The understanding, the intellect, is an active object or an objective activity, like the sunshine, the flowing water, the growing tree, the weathering stone or any other natural phenomenon. The understanding, the thinking, which takes place voluntarily or involuntarily in the human brain is also a perception, a perception of just as indubitable certainty as the most material perception. It cannot in the least shake our contention of the sense-perceptible nature of the thinking, knowing, intellectual activity, that we perceive this activity through the internal and not through the external sense. Whether a stone exists externally and the thought internally—what difference does this slight distinction make in the incontestable fact that both perceptions are of the same kind? Why should

---

Society, vol. 66, no. 2 (Summer, 2002): 203.
20. Ibid., 222.

not the thinking activity belong to the same category as the activity of the heart?[21]

This is not a vulgar materialism. Dietzgen recognized that mind is different from physical matter, but that it is not fundamentally different. Mind and matter are, in fact, equally part of the universal totality. He concluded that, as really existing things, mind and ideas share necessary connections with physical matter as part of their existence. That is, mind and ideas do not occur apart from physical reality; they must have an object—physical matter—in order to exist. Human reality cannot exist without this integration of both physical and mental phenomena in a system of relations that composes the entirety.[22] Our understanding of what comprises physical materiality is heavily constituted by our ideas. Furthermore, the constant creation, recreation, and development of the physically material world come largely as a result of the material effect of ideas and mental processes. If we adopt this notion of what constitutes materiality, the relationship of physical material to mental material may be conceived as a feedback loop with the physical and the mental codetermining each other. Furthermore, if one accepts this view, they see that that the phenomena of reality may not be reduced to discrete particulars, but must be understood as flexible conglomerations of relations that consist of both matter and ideas. Stephen Bales, for example, may be conceived of as more than an instance of the species Homo sapiens, but instead as a phenomenon consisting of physical matter, mind, and collections of ideas emanating both from him and about him, and only tangentially related to him. The appellation itself—Stephen Bales—adds something to the relationally constructed phenomena of Bales, i.e., the expression of Bales in the totality.

To summarize Dietzgen's understanding of dialectical materialism, we may posit the following statements concerning the world. First, we

---

21. Joseph Dietzgen, *The Positive Outcome of Philosophy: The Nature of Human Brain Work, Letters on Logic, The Positive Outcome of Philosophy*, trans. by W.W. Craik (Chicago: Charles H. Kerr & Company, 1906), 365.

22. Joseph Dietzgen. *The Nature of Human Brain Work: An Introduction to Dialectics* (Oakland, PA: PM Press 2010), 29.

conclude that reality is a unified material cosmos that consists of both physical and mental phenomena and that, for the cosmos, the totality constitutes the objective truth, and that the disparate phenomena (i.e., the physical, the mental, and combinations of these things as networks of relations) constitute partial and relative truths. Second, in the final analysis, the fundamental and generative basis of this unified material cosmos is a physical materiality which includes not only physical matter itself (i.e., atoms), but also includes both space (extension) and time (temporality).[23] Mind and its related phenomena—thought, ideas, ideologies, "spirit," etc.—result from this physical material reality. But, by assigning mind, regardless of its origination, an ontological status that is equivalent to that held by the phenomena traditionally assigned to physical reality, Dietzgen rendered such a sequence of origination, the "domino effect" causal model held by "eliminative" materialists,[24] to appear vulgar and deterministic. Even if mind is, in the last instance, rooted in and contingent upon physical reality, it is ontologically equivalent to physical matter in all other ways; that is, mind cannot be dismissed as being simply a byproduct of physical reality, to what the nineteenth-century physician and materialist Knowlton likened to the secretion of the bile as "a function of the liver, or the secretion of urine a function of the kidneys."[25] Mind cannot be written off as it is sometimes done by the eliminative materialists because, as Chalmers noted,

> […] it seems to be a further truth that we are conscious, and this phenomenon seems to pose a further explanandum that raises the interesting problems of consciousness. To flatly deny the further truth, or to deny without argument that there is a hard problem of consciousness over and above the easy problems, would be to make a highly counterintuitive claim that begs the important questions. This is not to say that

---

23. William James, *Essays in Radical Empiricism* (New York: Longmans, Green and Co., 1912), 4.

24. David J. Chalmers, "Consciousness and its Place in Nature," in *Blackwell Guide to the Philosophy of Mind* (Malden, MA: Blackwell, 2003), 109.

25. Charles Knowlton, *Elements of Modern Materialism* (Adams, MA: A. Oakey, 1829), 72.

highly counterintuitive claims are false, but they need to be supported by extremely strong arguments.[26]

Although the particular mode or expression of mind may be seen in the Spinozist sense as qualitatively different from physical matter, it is ultimately reducible to the same stuff, substance, or for lack of a better word, material. Mind, as a part of nature, is inherent and necessary in the integrative totality of reality and cannot be separated from nature as a totality without rendering the objective totality a crude and insufficient abstraction.

Not surprisingly, such a conception of the constitutive stuff of everything existing is plagued by the limitations of the terminology employed. Dietzgen recognized that the word matter is problematic because it implies concrete physical matter,[27] and hence one may conclude by extension that material and materialism are problematic as well. He explained reality as something akin to the idea of "substance" or "God" provided by Spinoza in that philosopher's *Ethics*, where Spinoza argued against mind/body dualism, writing that everything is the same substance, but may express itself in different modes or "affections."[28] Similarly, Dietzgen wrote that the "universe is the substance, substance in general, and all other substances are but its attributes. And this world-substance reveals the fact that the nature of things, the 'thing itself' [i.e., in the Kantian sense] as distinguished from its manifestations, is only a concept of the mind."[29] Whether it is called material, substance, or things like the ancient Greek philosophers' aêr or apeiron, Dietzgen held that all phenomena are equally existent and therefore equally materially real. This integrating and totalizing understanding of reality stresses the

---

26. Chalmers, "Consciousness and its Place in Nature, 109.

27. Joseph Dietzgen, *Some of the Philosophical Essays on Socialism and Science, Religion, Ethics, Critique-of-Reason and the World-at-Large*, eds. Eugene Dietzgen and Joseph Dietzgen, Jr., trans. M. Berr and T. Rothstein (Chicago, IL: Charles H. Kerr, 1917), 219.

28. Benedict Spinoza, *Ethics*, trans. W.H. White, rev. A.H. Stirling (Ware, UK: Wordsworth Editions, 2001), 5.

29. Dietzgen, *Nature of Human Brain Work*, 37.

transformative agency of the individual human subject and suggests that they have a responsibility to the totality because of this agency.

Some orthodox Marxists have accused Dietzgen's dialectical material monism of being not far removed from theoretical idealism. Lenin wrote in his *Materialism and Empirio-Criticism* that the tanner qualified as a dialectical materialist but that his thought was not "free from confusion."[30] Lenin concluded in his appraisal of Dietzgen that the philosopher was "nine-tenths a materialist [in the orthodox Marxist-Leninist sense] [who] never made any claims either to originality or to possessing a special philosophy distinct from materialism."[31] He appears to discount Dietzgen's overall contribution to dialectical materialism largely because of the latter thinker's "muddled" ideas (there is some truth to this accusation, as many of Dietzgen's writings are rather obscure), and Lenin's primary point of contention is that Dietzgen includes mind in his definition of material reality.[32] Much of this dismissive attitude towards this elevation of the ontological status of mind was a result of Lenin's project at the time, constructing a polemic against a form of bourgeois philosophy of science, the empirio-criticism of philosophers like Ernst Mach, that had been gaining popularity among the Russian Marxists and that had also adopted a neutral monism that was in ways similar to Dietzgen's cosmic dialectic. Nevertheless, Marx himself wrote about the materiality of thought, that "theory also becomes a material force once it has gripped the masses."[33]

Furthermore, this view of reality was by no means relegated only to Dietzgen's understanding of dialectical materialism, demonstrating its underlying appeal and perceived applicability. Although such monism may seem alien to many people today, neutral monism is not new to

---

30. V. I. Lenin, *Materialism and Empirio-Criticism: Critical Comments on a Reactionary Philosophy* (New York: International Publishers, 1972), 117.

31. Ibid., 253.

32. Ibid., 251.

33. Karl Marx, "A Contribution to the Critique of Hegel's Philosophy of Right," in *Early Writings*, trans. Rodney Livingstone and Gregor Benton (London: Penguin, 1992), 251.

the philosophy of science and continues to have proponents. The contemporary astrophysicist Max Tegmark, for instance, contended that mathematics is the basis of all reality, an idea that can be traced back 2500 years to Pythagoras. In Tegmark's iteration of neutral monism, he concluded that are our understandings are weighed down with semantic impedimenta: "all physics theories that I've been taught have two components: mathematical equations and 'baggage'–words that explain how the equations are connected to what we observe and intuitively understand."[34] In essence, this argument is also similar to Spinoza's idea of substance and its expression by means of various modes. Tegmark replaced substance with mathematics and mode with "baggage," updating philosophical monism with quantitative terminology that appeals to practitioners of the hard sciences. Indeed, neutral monism has represented an important stream in philosophical thought since Spinoza. Besides the work of the empirio-criticists (most notably that of the Vienna Circle), as well as late nineteenth-century philosophers like Haeckel, later "neutral monist" philosophies are seen in James's pragmatism and his philosophy of "pure experience,"[35] and the work of theorists like Alfred North Whitehead, Bertrand Russell, and C.D. Broad.

Dietzgen's dialectical materialism is a material monism that allows critical analysts to conceptualize a phenomenon's relationship with reality as a whole, a thoroughgoing and profoundly complete material whole that includes both matter and mind as ontologically equal.[36] Taking this route allows the critical analyst to view the MCAL and academic librarianship as a complex totality of both the physical and the mental.

---

34. Max Tegmark, *Our Mathematical Universe: My Quest for the Ultimate Nature of Reality* (New York: Alfred A. Knopf, 2014), 255.

35. See William James, *Essays in Radical Empiricism* (New York: Longmans, Green, 1922).

36. Middle class materialism, according to Dutch left communist theorist Anton Pannekoek in *Lenin as Philosopher: A Critical Examination of the Philosophical Basis of Leninism*, rev. ed, ed. Lance Byron Richey, Milwaukee: Marquette University Press, 2003), 83, is the dominant form of materialism found under capitalism and one that elevates the natural science view of reality as a physical reality and concludes that "everything spiritual is merely the product of material processes; ideas are the secretion of the brain."

It subverts the LIS quantitative/cognitive paradigm divide by making it whole as well as making it more than just the sum of its parts.

The Antagonistic Contradictions Found with the MCAL

The dialectical material monist considers material reality to be ultimate reality and an organic whole composed of both the physical and the mental. In the process, she affirms that this whole is composed of an immeasurable number of entities, phenomena, and the relationships between these things. All entities and phenomena, furthermore, are in constant movement and mutually condition one another, even if neither their motion nor their interconnections are readily apparent. That is, the individual material things that combine to form the unity are wholly dependent upon the unity. They are defined as much by the phenomena with which they move and interact, and without these relationships, they would cease to exist. So, unlike Platonic or Aristotelian views of nature, they cannot be reduced to any ultimate form, essence, or cause; only the totality may be considered in such a way. If a dissolution of the bonds that intermesh the part with the whole did occur (though it is not even possible), the part would have no reality, ceasing to be cognizable even as an idea. Furthermore, if anything is added to or subtracted from this material reality as a whole, or if anything within the material entirety is transformed in any way, the whole becomes something else, which it does ceaselessly. This ceaseless change is driven by the conflict of antagonistic contradictions.[37]

Considering that the movement of the whole is constant, dialectics has sometimes been described as a philosophy of becoming. If one remains ignorant of this constant transformation, reality appears to be cut and dry, and such a view allows for little reflexive understanding of the separation between understanding and ideology. As a result, progressive action is impeded and ultimately retarded. However, by

---

37. Vasilii Krapivin, *What is Dialectical Materialism?* (Moscow: Progress Publishers, 1985), 186-190.

studying and understanding these dialectical movements, critical analysts are able to account for what goes on in the world and realize that they themselves both define and are defined by the totalizing movement of the dialectical whole. Because of this necessary connection with the whole, individual things, such as the institution of the MCAL, essentially contain and reflect the oppositional tensions of the whole. Thus, by examining the individual object, say the MCAL, one is able to gain an understanding of its milieu, and at the same time, see the action of the milieu within the individual object, for as Lenin wrote, the dialectical whole is contained both in its entirety and within its parts: "Thus in any proposition we can (and must) disclose as in a 'nucleus' ('cell') the germs of all the elements of dialectics, and thereby show that dialectics is a property of all human knowledge in general."[38] The critical analyst comes to the conclusion, as a result of her intense study, that she may actively transform social reality by confronting and working to resolve contradictions.

Hegel identified the principle of the unity and conflict of opposites and used it to account for the inner workings of this constantly transforming reality. In this view, the encounter and clash of contradictory opposites becomes the engine of sociocultural and historical change and development.[39] This principle holds that reality is replete with contradictions that coexist and clash with one another, but that these same contradictions, depending on the sociocultural and historical context, many times necessitate one another. If there were no contradictions in reality, physical or social, we would be left with homogeneity and stasis; indeed, there would be no differentiation at all between things.

Obviously, human reality is not a roiling chaos of motion. Contradictory opposites often achieve and remain, at least for a time, in balance. These opposites' coexistence is reinforced by means of prevailing economic and cultural structures, violence, and hegemonic consent. So,

---

38. V. I. Lenin, *Philosophical Notebooks, Collected Works,* vol. 38, ed. Stewart Smith, trans. Clemence Dutt (Moscow: Progress Publishers, 1976), 359-361.

39. V. G. Afanasayev, *Dialectical Materialism* (New York: International Publishers, 1987), 11.

the endurance of the status quo may be traced to superstructural elements like government, organized religion, and the educational system; institutions that have been set into place in order to maintain these contradictions. Nonetheless, with materialist dialectics, nothing lasts forever besides transformation itself. Engels wrote that dialectics "reveals the transitory character of everything and in everything; nothing can endure before it except the uninterrupted process of becoming and passing away, of endless ascendency from the lower to the higher."[40] The relation between contradictions leads eventually to a point of crisis and a resulting transformation or becoming of reality into a new, qualitatively different totality. At a certain point, the opposing forces of a phenomenon become so inimical towards one another that one contradiction essentially overpowers and negates the other, resulting in a transformation because of the resolution of the contradiction and the creation of new contradictions. According to materialist dialectics, this process is repetitive and progressive, i.e., there are negations of negations, although such changes may certainly be marked by periods of torpor or the efforts of reactionary movements to roll back progress.[41] But, as the stress caused by the friction between the opposing elements of a phenomenon becomes too much for the status quo to bear, a crisis is reached in which these internal contradictions are resolved, resulting in the creation of a new unity in which elements of the former two remain but the entirety is qualitatively different and progressively refined. The results of these encounters may be immediate and obvious. Armed conflict, for example, pits persons against each other to violent ends, likely resulting in a new political landscape and distribution of power between adversaries. Other encounters may be subtle. Take, for example, a conversation between two librarians about the use possibilities of a newly acquired online index. This exchange may not appear to be particularly significant, but may mark the beginning of a significant

---

40. Friedrich Engels, *Anti-Dühring: Herr Eugen Dühring's Revolution in Science*, ed. C.P. Dutt, trans. Emile Burns (New York: International Publishers, 1939), 12.

41. Krapivin, *What is Dialectical Materialism?* 186.

collaboration and resulting innovation in LIS reference work. Both of the above examples are productive. A pitched battle is productive because the clash between opposing forces immediately brings a new condition of being into existence, both physical destruction and shifting power relations. The conversation between the two librarians likewise effects a change, usually a benign one that, if not particularly dramatic, is nonetheless a transformative interaction between competing ideas, and one that will result in future interactions and transformations. Both parties to the dialogue, willingly or not, consciously or not, present something to their counterpart that may be either blatantly or subtly contradictory to the other.

Because materialist dialectics is a philosophy of change, the contradictory opposites that exist within and between entities and phenomena are forever subject to transformation; they are not eternal. In the Marxist view, however, certain primary contradictions are endemic to every form of society and historical epoch, existing for the duration of the epoch and (itself contradictorily) acting as a motor for its continuance. For example, Marx identified a primary contradiction of the capitalist social formation in the opposition between the existence of a class tasked with creating value through their own labor, i.e., the proletariat, and a class of appropriators of this labor, the bourgeoisie. The latter class owns the means of production and has leveraged this ownership to continually exploit the labor of the proletariat for its own benefit. Although this contradiction—that so many have to work in order that a comparatively few number of people may live off the former group's production—is glaring, the situation persists despite multiple challenges and crises. Having identified this contradiction, the critical analyst may use it as a point of entry for understanding the various elements of capitalism, including the MCAL and academic librarianship, and how these elements and their internal and external contradictions unfold in relation to each other and in relation to the primary contradiction.

In Marxist theory, the resolution of contradictions is exemplified by a revolutionary paradigm shift in the prevailing mode of production. In this movement the proletariat brings down the capitalist system, in the process eliminating class distinctions. Such a transition is dialectical movement at its most dramatic. But what does the unity and conflict of opposites mean in regards to the MCAL, a modern institution that appears to be stable and is more often portrayed as an instrument of order (which it is) than as a revolutionary force (which it is as well)? The MCAL's contradictions appear to be much less epic in scale than the revolutionary struggle between proletariat and bourgeoisie. However, accepting dialectical materialism's underlying proposition that the unity of the social whole is defined by the interconnection of its parts, and that the individual object, as a result, contains the movement of the whole, the academic librarian must at some point consider the relationship of the MCAL to this social whole. Engaging in this sort of critical vigilance allows the academic librarian to remain intellectually honest concerning what they do as a professional. A combination of introspection and extrospection helps the librarian appreciate how her library and the larger cultural milieu interact with and condition each other. For instance, the MCAL both promotes political freedom and reproduces economic exploitation by reproducing the capitalist social formation. Democratic sentiments and preparation for informed participation in democratic political processes have long been associated with the operating ethos of academic libraries in capitalist social democracies. As an element of national educational infrastructure, MCALs work to prepare students to enter civic life and to realize and reproduce prevailing civic structures based upon institutionalized liberal democratic models. But, while many modern capitalist societies provide political suffrage to their citizenry, they do not provide economic equality, because of structural elements of society that they actively reproduce (and it is arguable as to how much the lack of the latter restricts the actuality of the political freedom component of the ethos). This contradiction surrounding democracy is also evidenced in the fact that the MCAL advocates for the Right to Access to Knowledge at the same time that it restricts access to knowledge. Article V of the ALA's *Library Bill of Rights* states that "a person's right to use a library should not be denied or abridged because of origin, age, background, or views."[42] As part of its role in support of democracy, American libraries, both public and academic, have acknowledged the necessity for both the freedom to read and intellectual freedom. In its *Intellectual Freedom Manual*, the ALA recognizes the connection between these ideas, stating in an interpretation of the *Library Bill of Rights* titled "The Universal Right to Free Expression" that "freedom of expression is an inalienable human right and the foundation for self-government,"[43] and that

> the American Library Association condemns any governmental effort to involve libraries and librarians in restrictions on the right of any individual to hold opinions without interference, and to seek, receive, and impart information and ideas. Such restrictions pervert the function of the library and violate the professional responsibilities of librarians.[44]

Other ALA interpretations of the Library Bill of Rights advocate free access to libraries for minors and identify physical and intellectual access to information as "a universal human right."[45] Nonetheless, the libraries attached to both private and public colleges and universities routinely do things like place restrictions on the access rights of non-affiliated and marginalized community users. They may also, whether unintentionally or otherwise, privilege corpuses of information that privilege the dominant culture over oppressed and emerging cultures.

Before considering what to do about the MCAL's antagonistic relations, I will reintroduce what I believe to be the MCAL's primary contradiction first mentioned in chapter 1: the MCAL is a site of both stasis and change, i.e., it conserves the status quo at the same time that

---

42. American Library Association, "Library Bill of Rights," in *Intellectual Freedom Manual*, 8th ed. (Chicago, IL: American Library Association, 2010), 49.

43. American Library Association, "Universal Right to Free Expression," in *Intellectual Freedom Manual*, 8th ed. (Chicago, IL: American Library Association, 2010), 195.

44. Ibid., 197.

45. American Library Association, "Free Access to Libraries for Minors: An Interpretation of the Library Bill of Rights," in *Intellectual Freedom Manual*, 8th ed. (Chicago, IL: American Library Association, 2010), 136-137.

it supports cultural and ideological foment. When I write about stasis or near synonyms like conservation, equilibrium, and counterpoise, I mean it as something quite different than motionlessness. Stasis is not the opposite of change, because in the dialectical worldview, there is no room for that sort of rigid immobility. Instead, I understand stasis to be an inflection and result of the oppositional application of progressive historical change, an opposing force that works actively in resistance to sociopolitical transformation. As such, stasis may be beneficial to humanity by preventing systemic decay; it may cancel out positive cultural and political transformation in order to preserve the status quo, or it may even result in a cultural and political regression.

The typical MCAL is a conservator of the sociocultural landscape in which it sits. The library performs this function in several important ways: it acts as a stockpile of the human knowledge which a society has determined valuable for both the society's continued existence and its future progress and therefore worthy of preservation; it maintains a hierarchically organized cadre of professional gatekeepers, the academic librarians, paraprofessionals, and administrative staff, to maintain and administrate this cache of information with the implicit understanding that they will do this as functionaries of the dominant paradigm; and it acts as an ideological state apparatus (ISA) like the family, church, and legal system. That is, the MCAL is an institution which supports and reproduces the relations of production of the dominant societal paradigm.[46] This role as an ISA is explored in more detail in the next chapter, but suffice it to say here that, if the reader understands the dominant paradigm's narrative concerning the legitimacy of the capitalist system and the status quo, they understand that it is not in the interest of the MCAL as an institution that is embedded in this system to upset this status quo.

In contradiction to the MCAL's conservative role is its function as a locus for antithetical, controversial, and fringe ideas, that is, as a

---

46. Louis Althusser, "Ideology and Ideological State Apparatuses (Notes Towards an Investigation)," in *Lenin and Philosophy and Other Essays*, trans. Ben Brewster (New York: Monthly Review Press), 100-101.

place of ideological struggle that is expressed in all types of recorded formats and further actualized through the library's supposedly neutral function as an engine for creating and disseminating knowledge. The fact is, however, that the majority of MCALs reflect, either intentionally and because of explicit ideological imperatives or because of their historical development, the prevailing thought, relations, and ideologies of its situational milieu.

One has only to look at the Western skew of the Library of Congress Subject Headings (LCSH) for evidence of this ideological bent. In his seminal 1971 book *Prejudices and Antipathies*, Sanford Berman published a scathing critique of the LCSH:

> [...] the LC list can "satisfy" parochial, jingoistic Europeans and North Americans, white-hued, at least nominally Christian (and preferably Protestant) in faith, comfortably situated in the middle and higher income brackets, largely domiciled in suburbia, fundamentally loyal to the Established Order, and heavily imbued with the transcendent, incomparable glory of Western civilization.[47]

Especially obnoxious examples flagged by Berman included "NEGRO CRIMINALS,"[48] "COMMUNISM—Jews,"[49] "ANARCHISM AND ANARCHISTS sa [see also] Terrorism,"[50] and "HOMOSEXUALITY xx [broader heading] Sexual perversion."[51] In a 2005 analysis of changes made per Berman's suggestions, Knowlton found that 80 of 225 suggested changes remain unchanged (all four of the examples given above were changed), with remaining bias concentrating around "Christian topics and unglossed terms relating to United States history and geography, which may simply be confusing to users outside the U.S."[52] That

---

47. Sanford Berman, *Prejudices and Antipathies: A Tract on the LC Subject Headings Concerning People* (Metuchen, NJ: Scarecrow Press, 1971), ix.
48. Ibid., 35.
49. Ibid., 61.
50. Ibid., 135.
51. Ibid., 182.
52. Steven A. Knowlton, "Three Decades since Prejudices and Antipathies;

changes did occur is a testament to counter-hegemonic action taken within the library community internally and outside of the Library of Congress. That this process is not yet finished after over 30 years is a testament to the turgidity of capitalism's ideological apparatuses.

Nonetheless, academic libraries are shot through with pockets of counter-hegemonic narratives that challenge the dominant cultural paradigm, as evidenced by the fact that they have long served as a hothouse for the development of controversial and confrontational ideas. Considering that the neoliberal narrative is currently ascendant in modern society, such hegemonically subordinated contradictory elements are held in check. They may even be used in the service of the dominant societal structure by maintaining the MCAL's role as a place open to contending ideas, while effectively quarantining them, for example, in "token" collections. Again, this is partially a function of the Library of Congress Classification system, which is biased towards U.S. American and Western subjects. It also results from the faux a-politicization of the MCAL and academic librarianship, with the ALA's professions of neutrality and acceptance of all points of view, when in reality academic libraries tend to reproduce the ideological terrain of the neoliberal capitalist society within which they operate. Like neoliberal society, the MCAL becomes a place where oppositional approaches to the dominant narrative, such as Marxism, feminism, and queer theory, are somewhat accepted but not often actively supported or promulgated. These oppositional approaches are ghettoized in the LIS world, just as they are within the larger culture; the bulk of institutional resources are used for maintenance of the status quo. Counter-hegemonic collections receive short shrift because the faculties they serve receive short shrift, and "overzealous" attempts to actively promote counter-hegemonic causes run afoul of the ALA's mandate to select items "for values of interest, information, and enlightenment of all the people of the community" and to present "all points of view concerning the problems and issues

---

A Study of Changes in the Library of Congress Subject Headings," *Cataloging & Classification Quarterly*, 40, no. 2 (2005): 128.

of our times [...]."⁵³ The sentiments of statements like these are well meaning, but they reduce the "neutral" academic librarian to the role of cypher for capitalist ideology. They mask the inherently political nature of all academic librarians, which will be explored in chapter 5 of this book, under a skein of false objectivity.

What is to Be Done? Harnessing the MCAL through Understanding Its Relations

Ernst Untermann defined Dietzgen's version of materialist dialectics as "a method of expression which aims to portray the natural movement in the universe."⁵⁴ The MCAL itself is a metaphor for this conception of reality. If we observe the MCAL in the same way that we view the totality of social reality, we discover a multiplicity of phenomena that is interactive, mutable, transmutable, and revolutionary. The scientific communication occurring at and through the MCAL mirrors the dialectical nature of the cosmos. Where does the MCAL fit into this paradigmatic approach to reality and how might this conception of reality be employed to subvert and change the contradictions found in the library? The library is a totality that is defined by the many of physical objects, information resources, patrons, information workers, and other people that work in it or are associated with it in some way. These individual materialities are never static. Users, user needs, library personnel, and resources are not immobile but are in a constant state of transition. The MCAL is always the sum of its component parts, at the same time that the totality represents something more than a mere summation. Phenomena constantly fold into each other to define a totality that is relative and provisional. Ollman argued that Marx adopted a philosophy of internal relations as the philosophical grounding for his critiques of capitalism, concluding that the "relation is the irreducible

---

53. American Library Association, "Library Bill of Rights," in *Intellectual Freedom Manual*, 8th ed. (Chicago, IL: American Library Association, 2010), 56.
54. Ernest Untermann, *Science and Revolution* (Chicago: Kerr, 1910), 193.

minimum for all units in Marx's conception of social reality,"[55] and that dialectic is the study of systems of relations. Everything is connected with everything else through both internal and external relations. Everything is both divisible and combinable in an infinite number of ways, i.e., different congeries of matter and ideas, from the smallest units, a single grain of sand, an atom, a thought; to people, groups of people, groups of people and machines, groups of people and a body of ideas, institutions, societies; all the way up to the totality, the ultimate thing, the total reality, the cosmos. Therefore, literally any *thing* (recognizing that absolutely nothing is a singularity in either a physical or ideal sense) may be considered and analyzed as a relation, no matter how minute or how expansive. The previous section introduced this monistic interpretation of dialectical material reality. This interpretation may be encapsulated in the following four basic propositions:

1. Everything determines every thing;

2. every thing determines Everything;

3. every thing determines *every thing*; and

4. *every thing* determines every thing.

That is, if one recognizes the universe as a singular objective totality that is comprised of an infinite number of subjective but transmutable and related individual phenomena, then it follows that the cause of every individual thing is the Everything, the entire cosmos; the existence and character of the cosmos is likewise determined by the constant congress and transformation of every individual thing with every other individual thing.

Therefore, to adopt the positions of both Dietzgen and Ollman, any change to any phenomenon—be it an internal change or a change effected through interaction with other phenomena—no matter how

---

55. Bertell Ollman, *Dance of the Dialectic: Steps in Marx's Method* (Urbana, IL: University of Illinois Press, 2003), 25.

minute this change may be, transforms every other phenomena or spawns new phenomena. In the process, every change to every individual phenomenon changes the universe in its totality. The interconnectedness of all things as relations means that an individual's existence (and one can see how using the term "individual" in this context becomes problematic), and the situation of that existence, works in some manner to determine the identity of every other individual thing. This co-determinacy, furthermore, extends throughout history, with past relations mediating the composition of present relations and present relations influencing how we shape the past in our cognitions and ideologies. Assuming this standpoint means that the critical analyst may identify the part within the whole and conversely the whole within the part. That is, she may see how they contain each other in their entirety. This is because if all things are bound up in and codetermined by all other things, then even the smallest units of analysis, as Ollman noted in his analysis of Hegel, are actually a microcosm of all the other elements comprising the universe.[56] The individual unit of analysis is a relation that is codetermined by all other relations past and present. The MCAL is therefore also determined by *all other relations past and present.* As a result, any subunit of the totality becomes a perspectival window into understanding the whole, while attempts at understanding the whole,[57] or a massive institution like the MCAL as a unit of analysis, allows the critical analyst to better understand the flexible multiplicity of its constitutive elements.

The four positions listed above may be further simplified into two propositions:

1. *every thing* codetermines every thing

2. Everything codetermines every thing

---

56. Ollman, *Dance of the Dialectic*, 41.
57. Ibid., 75.

Finally, this two-part conception of reality may be summarized with a four-word formulation that has an Eastern philosophical flavor: What *is*, is everything. That is, because of the interpenetrating nature of the totalizing conception of reality, everything that exists, physical and mental, refracts everything else existing. What *is* history *is* you; what *is* you *is* me; what *is* my history *is* you; what *is* us *is* you *is* them *is* everything, ad infinitum. This is a complex understanding of reality, but by taking such a perspective critical analysts become acutely aware of the codeterminations and consequences of what they analyze. They also become acutely aware of the codeterminative relations in which they themselves participate as well as the consequences of their own actions within these relations. Such awareness gives the analyst insight into their place in a political economy of the library, and it requires that they evaluate the effects of their agency as professional librarians. Assuming a dialectical material monist perspective will likely have a radicalizing effect on analysts' understanding of their profession.

I have posited that the MCAL and academic librarianship are contextually grounded, material phenomena that develop through the movement of history. Such a dialectical approach to thought and action provides the academic librarian with theoretical tools to better understand the phenomena that surround the library and librarianship in terms of the unity of the whole, i.e., the totality of material social existence past and present, as well as gives them a means for envisioning and effecting a positive, more equitable future in which the MCAL, or some other iteration of the academic library, remains a vital part. By means of dialectical materialism, the critical analyst is afforded a holistic vantage point that both allows for and encourages meaningful change. This is not an easy task because it requires the analyst to think expansively about the many things involved in how a phenomenon expresses itself, but it beats simplistic abstractions because the dialectical approach's commitment to constant critique means that the analyst refuses to seriously entertain one-dimensional explanations and allows for understanding reality in ways that are much richer and deeper.

The purpose of the critical analysis helps to determine the type of things (phenomena, substance, processes, etc., but all of which comprise relations) selected for the analysis, and it determines the complexity of these relations. As a result, some analyses are not worth pursuing because the relations are too minute or obscure. The MCAL, however, is in no way minute or obscure. In purely quantitative terms, U.S. and Canadian academic libraries are cultural and economic powerhouses. According to the *ARL Statistics, 2011-2012 Survey*, the Association of Research Libraries member libraries had expenditures of almost $4.5 billion.[58] These 125 ARL member libraries are also major employers of physical and intellectual labor, employing 12,714 professional staff and 15,452 support staff.[59] In 2011-2012 alone, these libraries facilitated 8,452,307 reference transactions and 347,075,987 regular (non-federated) searches.[60] There are also hundreds of non-ARL libraries in the U.S. and Canada, and when one considers the network of all academic libraries worldwide, one begins to see the vast institutional power of the MCAL. As a massive global presence that wields great influence, the MCAL plays an important part in codetermining modern life. It takes part in relations with socially determinative institutions like education and politics.

Adopting the perspective that reality is divisible in multiple ways, the critical analyst may consider the MCAL from many different perspectives that center upon particular conjunctions of relations between phenomena. For example, relations may be constructed between the MCAL as a broadly conceived institution (a unit of analysis that itself consists of multitudinous internal and external relations) and other broad social institutions:

- MCAL ←[relation]→ System of public education;

---

58. Association of Research Libraries, *ARL Statistics, 2011-2012 Survey*, eds. M. Kyrillidou, S. Morris, and G. Roebuck (Washington, DC: Association of Research Libraries, 2013), 6.

59. Ibid., 38.

60. Ibid., 39.

- MCAL ←→ Popular culture;
- MCAL ←→ High-brow culture;
- MCAL ←→ Religious system;
- MCAL ←→ Political establishment;
- MCAL ←→ Mass media;
- MCAL ←→ Neo-liberal society (as a whole);

In addition, relations may be conceived in terms of more specific conjunctions:

- MCAL ←→ Academic librarians;
- MCAL ←→ Paraprofessional staff;
- MCAL ←→ Faculty users;
- MCAL ←→ Community users;
- MCAL ←→ Non-users;
- MCAL ←→ Homeless people;
- MCAL ←→ Library vendors;
- Academic librarians ←→ Paraprofessional staff;
- Library Vendors ←→ Homeless people

These relations may be identified and analyzed ad infinitum, with identification and analysis ultimately being a function of the critical analyst's practical goals. The one-to-one relations above are given here for simplicity's sake. Relations may, in fact, be expressed using a potentially infinite number of terms. For example, a more complex relation might be conceived as MCAL ←→ Library vendors ←→ Political establishment.

Relations like these represent potential ways to organize inquiry into concrete material interactions. They work as windows into observing the totality by privileging a facet of the total reality (e.g., the MCAL) in a way that requires the critical analyst to see how other circumscribable relations organize in respect to it. For example, when viewing the totality through the MCAL as a primary facet of the totality, we can then investigate how something like organized religion expresses in this particular relational articulation. We might next consider how a phenomenon like library anxiety fits into this model. Performing such analyses is something like going down the proverbial rabbit hole, for understanding one relation may require that the critical analyst expand the scope of her analysis to include other relations that have emerged during the critique, or that she deconstruct certain relations in order to further understand them.

My own research has centered on the MCAL's religious legacies. I have argued that the academic library is in fact a crypto-temple that incorporates religious symbols inherited from the ancient and feudal social formations to create an ideological structure that reflects and maintains the capitalist mode of production.[61] I argued in this research that overt and covert religious symbolism persists in the materiality of the MCAL and that this symbolism aids in the reproduction of neoliberal capitalism. Broadly conceived, the relation investigated may be represented as MCAL ←→ Religious system ←→ Neoliberal capitalism ←→ Feudalism, where all of these elements interact both synchronically and diachronically to codetermine each other and ultimately to support the continued existence of the capitalist social formation. Viewing these interactions gives the analyst insight into all of these elements, but considering that the MCAL is her focal point, that node of the relation remains of particular interest in her research and helps to guide the direction of her research and to focus her analysis and praxis.

Alternatively, the religious relationship with the MCAL may be specified into any number of relationships such as Academic librarians ←→ Religious system ←→ Neoliberal capitalism ←→ Library materials

---

61. Stephen Bales, "Academic Library as Crypto-Temple," *Class and Librarianship: Essays at the Intersection of Information, Labor and Capital*, eds. Erik Estep and Nathaniel Enright (Sacramento, CA: Library Juice, forthcoming).

theft, etc. Again, the specific relationship that is eventually selected for critical analysis is ultimately determined by the practical goals of the critical analyst. That is, if I am primarily concerned with the MCAL as crypto-temple as it affects homeless people, I will use this relation as a lens for orienting homeless people to the crypto-temple. Although this methodology deals with abstractions (religion being a particularly notorious example of abstraction), all of the abstractions must remain concrete. That is, instead of reducing any particular relation to a one-sided eternal that is a thing in itself, an abstraction is always used as a vantage point for viewing all other relations of interest within their historical context, and all abstractions must be considered as linked in some manner to all other abstractions. This procedure requires that the analyst move back and forth between different parsings of abstracted relationships in order to map the mutually dependent whole in as detailed a representation of material reality as possible, i.e., as what Ollman referred to as Marx's concept of the "thought concrete,"[62] or the reproduction in the mind of perceived material reality in a way that foregrounds certain elements for the purpose of understanding their relationships to other elements without losing context. Ollman quite effectively described the process of understanding "concrete" abstractions using the symphony as an explanatory metaphor. "In listening to a concert, for example, we often concentrate on a single instrument or recurring theme and then redirect our attention elsewhere. Each time this occurs, the whole music alters, new patterns emerge, and each sound takes on a different value."[63] This sort of analysis is not an easy task, but it is one that is productive because it works to map a material whole for both thought and physical matter. Using this approach to map the MCAL allows the critical analyst to pinpoint problematic elements in need of being addressed.

---

62. Ollman, *Dance of the Dialectic*, 60.
63. Ibid., 61.

Know Your Opponent

This dialectics of total reality, at its most basic, may be seen as the active interplay of action and reaction. All of reality is material action, and as I have argued, everything that we do affects everything else. Non-dialectical thinking is often unreflective thinking. If we adopt a dialectical material monist viewpoint, we can begin to see how such unreflective thought becomes fixed in structures and processes. We should eschew "traditional" concepts like "library neutrality" as nothing but weak attempts at validating an immobility that does not exist. The MCAL reflects assumed ontological positions and their related epistemologies in multiple ways, e.g., in the manner in which research is typically conducted for implementing the resources that the academic library provides access to; in how the library itself is studied and understood; and in the way academic librarians and library paraprofessionals approach their work, that is, how they implement and help to perpetuate the library as a social institution. To fully account for the massive scope and effects of the MCAL as a social institution, it is necessary to adopt an orientation towards the institution that allows for the consideration of the multiplicity of phenomena that are taken as traditionally part of the academic library, as well as those phenomena that are typically seen as falling outside of the sphere of the library.

Considering that the progressive application of dialectics to reality is a political undertaking, it is incumbent upon the dialectician to thoroughly know their opposition. As a constitutive organ of society, the MCAL has immense reach, and its sociocultural influence can be traced to sectors of capitalist (as well as non-capitalist) institutions and phenomena that would otherwise not be considered or be seen as falling within its purview, especially when approaching the topic from traditional positivist, idealist, or qualitative empiricist methods. A dialectical materialist monist approach accounts for the recursive nature of social phenomena, meaning that the influences of the sociocultural environment as a totality and as particular phenomena upon the MCAL are accounted for in terms of both social particularities and totalities.

As an institution based in capitalism, the MCAL shares the basic contradictions found in the social whole, the conflict between a class of producers of value and a class that appropriates this value. As described in this chapter, this conflict is expressed in multiple ways: both advocating and restricting access to potentially liberating knowledge, preventing the creation of such knowledge, promoting political freedom at the expense of economic freedom, and supporting the status quo while being the locus of social foment. Although these contradictions are at their basis antagonistic, their stability is maintained by the overdetermining nature of the relationships found between the MCAL and the social whole. As a result, the counter-hegemonic tendencies found within the MCAL, such as the library's role as an impetus for revolutionary transformation, its material incorporation of radical political ideas in the form of counter-hegemonic literature, and its role in the production of counter-hegemonic knowledge, both in the form of material information and cognitions, are often stymied. The next chapter looks in more detail at the MCAL's role in supporting stasis with a view towards making change.

Chapter 4

THE MCAL AND IDEOLOGY

If we accept the dialectical principle of the constant transformation of everything and every thing, then why do certain elements of society seem so slow to actually change? How do we make sense of historical stasis? The MCAL contains an important contradiction that potentially impacts our futures. At the same time that the institution contains within itself the infinite possibility for change, it represents a stability grounded in history and the cultural and political authority that history imparts. The MCAL contains revolution and reaction simultaneously. It voices humanity's capacity for wild, unchecked aggrandizement at the same time that it expresses humanity's capacity for preservation. In its simplest formulation, this contradiction may be stated as "the MCAL is motion and stasis"; it is these two material forces' confrontation in time and space. Regardless of the specific historical and sociocultural formations in which academic libraries or their precursors have operated, whether or not we consider the MCAL using traditional historical materialist categories like ancient, feudal, and capitalist, libraries have always performed these functions of movement and conservation. Retrogression comes as the result of force, whether this force is explicitly or implicitly realized, whether it is direct or indirect. As such, stasis may be beneficial to humanity by preventing systemic decay; it may cancel out positive cultural and political transformation in order to preserve the status quo, or it may even result in a cultural or political atavism. While the previous chapter focused primarily on the change polarity of the MCALs primary contradiction, I will now shift the conversation to more fully discuss the opposite term, stasis.

These outcomes occur because, as a species, human beings tend to be neurotic about change and uncertainty. The library is one fruit of this anxiety. The recognition of the limitedness of biological human memory led humans to develop sophisticated physical tools to safeguard the products of their intellectual labors. This impulse to fix things for (hopefully) infinitude extends into many other aspects of our realities, and what we cannot fix through physical possession and control, we do so through the process of simple abstractions that neutralize history by attempting to minimize change, turning past, present, and future into an eternal now. Marx and Engels said as much in *The German Ideology* when they critiqued the capitalist ideology of mid-nineteenth-century Europe, writing that dominant ideas are transformed into "eternal law."[1] The reigning socio-political paradigm reinforces its realities as ultimate truth by adding to their perceived normality, and the society's hegemonic institutions buttress and reproduce this normality as part of a natural order. The transformation of the dominant ideology into articles of faith and the reduction of processes to rigid generalizations strip history of its rich diachronic and synchronic consanguine relations. This process has important sociocultural consequences.

Acknowledging the MCAL's status as a principal conservator of dominant culture, this chapter employs the term "hegemonic academic libraries" to describe academic libraries in all historical periods. I argue that, in performing their work as ideological institutions, hegemonic academic libraries help to stabilize social historical structures, with neoliberal capitalism being the current, particularly volatile form of such social historical structures. Wittingly or not, those working at the MCALs help to fulfill this function on behalf of the dominant societal class's interests, unless they achieve theoretical consciousness of the underlying circumstances that they are supporting. This contention,

---

1. Karl Marx and Friedrich Engels, *The German Ideology* (Amherst, NY: Prometheus Books, 1998), 67.

that MCALs work as a sort of cultural and intellectual ballast for capitalist societies, does not ignore the fact that there are thousands of well-intentioned academic librarians engaging in good work at their libraries, but that ideology is materially present in the deep structure of Western educational systems, and that because of this the MCAL does not fully support the best interests of many people. Instead, as a brace for capitalism, the hegemonic MCAL *qua* ideological apparatus acts as a release valve for tensions found in capitalist societies. The MCAL works to curb capitalism's anarchistic tendencies, and it works as an engine for reproducing existing exploitative class structures, thus supporting the social formation's continued survival. This role is mystified in the ideological forms reproduced by the academic library and it may be ignored by those people working in the place. Nonetheless, it possesses a significant material force. This chapter further explores the notion that the MCAL is a materially realized ideological mechanism embedded in a neoliberal capitalist social formation, and as a sort of structural scaffolding it works to dehumanize masses of people by supporting neoliberalism in the same instance that it is a potent tool for education, knowledge creation, and social change.

Following a brief discussion of the concept of ideology, I explore ideological structures of pre-modern proto-libraries and early libraries to shed light upon similar social relations within the modern neoliberal capitalist institutions.[2] I argue that academic libraries have operated as (re)generators of the dominant social relations in all historical eras. Following this, I then discuss how the MCAL perpetuates these class ideological functions in the modern milieu, making the library an effective instrument for stunting dialectical progress. This discussion sets the stage for the next chapter, which investigates the dialectical

---

2. I use the term "proto-libraries" to mean information institutions that existed in the ancient world prior to the Great Library of Alexandria (founded ca. 300 BCE). I use the term "early libraries" to refer to the Great Library of Alexandria and the libraries which followed it, up until the beginnings of capitalism.

potential of academic librarians to move the hegemonic MCAL towards counter-hegemony.

The Enduring Problem of Ideology

The *Oxford English Dictionary* defines ideology as a "systematic scheme of ideas, usually relating to politics, economics, or society and forming the basis of action or policy; a set of beliefs governing conduct. Also: the forming or holding of such a scheme of ideas."[3] Marx and Engels used the term to denote a false consciousness of reality, a historically and culturally conditioned distortion of the actual material relations between people and between people and social phenomena, e.g., the relations between individuals and groups and institutions like the political system or the MCAL. Freeden described this obfuscation as happening "through ideological sleight of hand and through fetishizing (bestowing a sacred and mystifying status on) commodities and the markets in which they circulated [...]."[4] According to classical Marxism, such ideological distortions are ultimately generated and maintained by the dominant mode of production. The consciousness that an individual obtains from their immersive indoctrination into their social environment is typified by a view of reality that many times falls prey to idealism, which we have seen that, when carelessly abstracted, is a viewpoint that can divorce the discernment of reality from history and that can lead to the conclusion that *things just are like they are*. According to Marx and Engels, again from *The German Ideology*:

> In the whole conception of history up the present this real basis of history has either been totally disregarded or else considered as a minor matter quite irrelevant to the course of history. History must, therefore, always be written according to an extraneous standard; the real

---

3. "ideology, n. 4". OED Online. September 2014. Oxford University Press. http://www.oed.com.lib-ezproxy.tamu.edu:2048/view/Entry/91016?redirectedFrom=ideology.

4. Michael Freeden, *Ideology: A Very Short Introduction* (Oxford, UK: Oxford University Press, 2003), 7.

production of life appears as non-historical, while the historical appears as something separated from ordinary life, something extra-superterrestrial. With this the relation of man to nature is excluded from history and hence the antithesis of nature and human history is created.[5]

Marx and Engels contrasted this idea of consciousness sans historical perspective with the idea of a supposedly non-ideological, scientific approach to understanding social relationships by means of Marxist analysis. The critical analyst achieves a scientific understanding of the class content of human relations by which these relations are seen "as they really are and happened."[6] Assuming the material conception of reality, the Marxist analyst is able to identify symptoms of this false consciousness as it manifests itself in capitalist institutions, social relations, and cultural phenomena.

This orthodox Marxist conception of ideology has definite limitations, one being that many non-Marxist ideologies, for example those put forth by the "bourgeois" social sciences, provide varying degrees of access to understandings of a society's underlying social currents and relationships. This contention is born out constantly by the practical successes of psychology and sociology. At the same time, historical instantiations of Marxist theory as practice have proven themselves to be just as ideologically tainted as right wing ideology in the sense Arendt wrote about in her *Origins of Totalitarianism*. If, as Arendt wrote, ideology is "quite literally what its name indicates; it is the logic of an idea,"[7] and if one agrees that any set of ideas is ultimately founded on historically and culturally based systems of reasoning, then scientific Marxism is as much an ideology as any other.

Regardless of the oftentimes justified critiques of classical Marxist definitions of ideology, Marx and Engel's theories are valuable because they identified human perception and understanding of reality as

---

5. Marx and Engels, *German Ideology*, 62-63.

6. Ibid., 45.

7. Hannah Arendt, *The Origins of Totalitarianism* (San Francisco, CA: Harcourt Brace, 1973), 471.

mediated and defined by things beyond mere sensory input. The two men saw the construction of lived reality as necessarily including material existence, action, and interaction of both explicit (i.e., immediately conscious to the subject) and implicit (i.e., unconscious to the subject yet lived materially by them) historically determined ideas and relationships that focus and fix our experience of "the way things are." This is good news; it means that one need not be resigned to the conclusion that reality is rigidly deterministic and excludes independent thought or action. If the critical analyst cultivates a dialectical approach to understanding her world, she will develop an understanding of the dialectical nature of ideology as an entirety, as well as the nuances of the dominant ideology of the society in which she lives. That is, the analyst will gain insight into the ways that history, culture, and she herself work in concert to continually create and fix her reality and the reality of the communities which she serves, as well as how these same things result in repressive social constructs' generally persistent nature. Realizing and coming to terms with her reflexivity in relation to the construction of her environment, she may then orient herself consciously and critically to this socially constructed reality. Essentially, knowing that everyone—herself included—has an ideology allows the critical analyst to continually refine her understanding of social reality so as to better conform her practice towards developing a model of reality that is both rational and encourages equitable relationships.

At its most basic, dialectical material monism may be seen as the active interplay of action and reaction. All of reality is material action and, as I argued previously, everything that we do affects everything else. As is the case with any historically situated system of sociocultural production, neoliberal capitalism persists with the aid of a historically specific and determined ideological hardpan. The ideologies found in modern societies may be conceived of as being embodied in different modalities. Ideologies may be specific, individually adhered to, and explicitly acknowledged creeds, dogmas, theories, or personal philosophies. They are consciously recognized and intentionally adopted by a subject at varying levels of conscious commitment, as is the case when someone joins a political organization like the GOP, the Democratic Party, or the Democratic Socialists of America; a labor organization like the United Auto Workers, the International Workers of the World, or the AFSCME Library Union; or when someone identifies with a religious ideology such as Christianity or Islam.

Ideologies may also consist of overarching, "ambient" frameworks that humans both construct and are in turn constructed by as a result of the material historical conditions in which they are embedded. That is, an ideological structure can support a general worldview or *Weltanschauung* in the sense put forth by Mannheim, as a "total ideology" that is implicitly realized and lived by people.[8] Kettler and Meja described such total ideologies as a "concept designating a style of thought inherent in a social and historical location,"[9] a concept that is also more or less analogous to Žižek's understanding of the Lacanian "symbolic order," the "elaborate set of inter-subjective and trans-subjective contexts into which individual human beings are thrown at birth (along the lines of Heideggerian *Geworfenheit*), a pre-existing order preparing places for them in advance and influencing the vicissitudes of their ensuing lives."[10] Total ideology, therefore, is essentially inseparable from physical reality itself. As per the thought of Dietzgen and later thinkers like Althusser, it is materially embedded into all of the various material human social and cultural institutions. Both total ideology and self-selected political ideologies can and do exist simultaneously within the same individual. Someone can, for instance, be a card carrying member of the communist party at the same time that she is steeped in, and possibly unreflectively so, the neoliberal total ideology. Such concurrences illustrate the ability

---

8. Karl Mannheim, *Ideology & Utopia: An Introduction to the Sociology of Knowledge* (San Diego, CA: Harcourt. 1936), 36.

9. David Kettler and Volker Meja, *Karl Mannheim and the Crisis of Liberalism: The Secret of These New Times* (New Brunswick, NJ: Transaction Publishers, 1995), 78.

10. *Stanford Encyclopedia of Philosophy*, s.v. "Jacques Lacan," by Adrian Johnston, accessed January 13, 2014, http://plato.stanford.edu/entries/lacan/.

of capitalism to adapt to seemingly incompatible worldviews, and its ability to incorporate oppositional ideas.

Ideologies also work to define each other through their relationships with each other. Part of the GOP's ideology, for instance, rests on values which are influenced by aspects of America's *Weltanschauung*, like the culture's strong historical cultural Protestant influences and Protestantism's lionization of concepts like moral absolutes and work discipline.[11] I do not mean to say here that the Protestant influence does not hold sway on other political parties, just that it is a notable force within the ideology of Western traditional conservatism and particularly the American Republican Party. Likewise, the GOP's material actions, e.g., their political operations, feed back into Americans' construction of their realities, with things like policy and propaganda influencing the constitution of their total world views. American political groups like the Democratic Socialists of America are, despite their radical leftist platforms, also grounded in the American capitalist *Weltanschauung*, although they tend towards being more aware of this foundation and may adopt measures to challenge the ideological undertow.

The ideological power infused into and wielded by social institutions is in no way a unique facet of capitalist society. Socially materialized ideology has persisted throughout all preceding periods of human history, including the ancient and the feudal modes of social organization. In some capacity, academic libraries have always operated as ideological mechanisms supporting exploitative, and thus ultimately conservative, societal infrastructures. The MCAL is a materialized ideological structure that works to temper the push and pull of dialectical movement, both within the MCAL as institution and within the society as a whole. However, unlike her predecessors, the modern academic librarian is in a unique position of strength, even though she is many times unaware of this position and must be made conscious of this strength. Advances

---

11. See Brian R. Farmer, *American Political Ideologies: An Introduction to the Major Systems of Thought in the 21st Century* (Jefferson, NC: McFarland & Company, 2006), 46; N.T. Feather, "Protestant Ethic, Conservatism, and Values," *Journal of Personality and Social Psychology* 46, no. 5 (1984): 1138-1139.

in social thought, particularly those theoretical advances coming out of the voluminous body of work produced by Marxist and post-Marxist critical and cultural thinkers, give the academic librarian *cum* critical analyst a methodological point of entry for her analysis into the MCAL that accounts for ideology as a facet of social being. This body of work also provides the critical analyst with the necessary tools to critique the conservative torpor of an institution composed as much of materially actualized ideas as it is by bricks, mortar, and technology, while arming her to prod the institution out of its historically and culturally produced malaise. The trick to all of this is in first developing a radical social consciousness, one that accounts for the prevailing ideology, in addition to the will and practical capacity to act progressively counter to it.

The anthropologist Levi-Strauss felt that understanding the timeless structure of myth, synchronic time, requires that one also understand myth as process, as existing within diachronic time:

> By getting at what we call *harmony*, they would find out that an orchestral score, in order to become meaningful, has to be read diachronically along one access—that is, page after page, and from left to right—and also synchronically along the other axis, all the notes which are written vertically making up one gross constituent unit, i.e. one bundle of relations.[12]

The same methodological approach applies to the study of human institutions as the symbols and loci of myth. Humans are historical beings. Ideology, as a result, cannot be escaped; it is inseparable from human consciousness and human reality.[13] The following discussion adopts a historicist approach to ideology. That is, it assumes that having ideology—whether it is explicitly or implicitly held—is a trait shared by every human engaged in social relationships, that ideologies, while mythological in form, arise from and are bound to historical context, and that they develop over time and as a consequence of changing

---

12. Claude Lévi-Strauss, "The Structural Study of Myth," *Journal of American Folklore* 68, no. 270 (1955): 432.

13. Terry Eagleton, "Ideology and Its Vicissitudes," in *Mapping Ideology*, ed. Slavoj Žižek (London: Verso, 1994), 180.

material conditions. Furthermore, I operate under the assumption that theoretical understanding of the world is rooted in ideological milieu and that the accuracy of a theory, and therefore the practical sufficiency of an operational ideological standpoint, is confirmed by conscious and reflexive praxis.[14]

Tracing the Hegemonic Academic Library through History

Libraries have existed in one form or another for thousands of years, for nearly as long as the existence of recorded language. They seem to be the inevitable consequence and material expression (both physical and mental) of the human impulse to organize their realities as well as the human impulse to increase their labor productivity by developing technological instruments as extensions of themselves. In the case of the library, humans have created an extension of their cognitive processes and memories that serves practical, ideological, and fetishistic functions. During their long history, libraries have supported academic and scholarly purposes as well as administrative, archival, and religious roles. In fact, many times throughout history there has been little clear distinction between these roles, even within the same individual institutions. The people who ran the proto-libraries and early libraries, the ancient scribes and early librarians, also tended to personify and actualize these functions. An ancient proto-library worker might be simultaneously a scholar, a bureaucrat, an archivist, and a cleric. It is only recently that libraries have deliberately sought to separate out these raison d'êtres; truly secular academic libraries have existed for only the last few centuries as institutions that are more or less overtly dedicated to one or two primary functions, although there is most always some overlap with the other categories.

By bolstering the *Weltanschauung* and therefore reinforcing the status quo, MCALs serve the same basic ideological purposes as their historical

---

14. Ibid., 212.

precursors even if their stated purposes and missions might suggest otherwise. The difference between the pre-modern information institutions and the modern capitalist libraries, however, is that the preceding modes of production, the ancient and the feudal, did not so heavily obscure the social relations as does the capitalist *Weltanschauung*.[15] In the preceding social formations, members of society such as the ancient slave and the feudal serf were likely more cognizant of understanding the social positions. This transparency required that the dominant forces reinforce their positions of power with a higher degree of undisguised violence and oppression.

Therefore, until the ascendance of the capitalist mode of production and the development of the institutions and ideologies that characterize that social formation, libraries have unapologetically acted as a sort of ideological scaffolding for the societies in which they operated. This social function is evidenced through their unambiguous administrative and religious purposes. In many ancient civilizations, e.g., the Sumerian and Egyptian, the proto-libraries were run by elites for elites. Even the so-called "public libraries" of civilizations such as Greece and Rome were not public in the sense that we use the word today; they were exclusionary in that a large portion of the population, the slaves and possibly the plebeians, were restricted in their use them.[16] This relative transparency of the pre-modern institutions' roles contrasts directly with the popular image of the modern secular MCAL, which, with its internal relations heavily obscured by the comprehensive reification that

---

15. Bertell Ollman, "Market Mystification in Capitalist and Market Socialist Societies," Dialectical Materialism: The Writings of Bertell Ollman, accessed January 1, 2015, http://www.nyu.edu/projects/ollman/docs/market_mystification.php.

16. T. Keith Dix argued in "'Public Libraries in Ancient Rome: Ideology and Reality," *Libraries & Culture* 29, no. 3 (1994): 290, that in the case of the Roman "public" libraries' reality, the libraries did not correspond to general access and that although public readings may have been held, access may have been limited to a select few: "given the economic, social, and cultural restrictions which bound most individuals in the ancient world, it seems safe to say that only a very small number are likely ever to have availed themselves to peruse the volumes in a public library."

is typically associated with the capitalist mode of production, appears to transcend unseemly ideological considerations altogether. The MCAL has, in most cases, discarded or sublimated manifest political ideologies, although those certainly still exist in it, but it nonetheless maintains and reproduces the basic capitalist *Weltanschauung*. As a result, MCALs may come across as factotums or cure-alls, as instruments for engaging in a range of positive outcomes limited only by their patrons' and staffs' imaginations. Pre-capitalist proto-libraries and early libraries offer a window into the persistent relations and internal contradictions that were inherited by the MCAL.

Proto-libraries and early libraries have often served the interests of the ruling factions and dominant socioeconomic classes of the societies in which they were built. From a Marxist perspective, the majority of proto-libraries and early libraries, like all major state institutions, have to some extent worked against the interests of subaltern classes at the same moment that they may have ostensibly worked for them. At times the dominant class entities of individual societies have consisted of an individual ruler, a ruling family, a small powerful junta, or an elite class, as was often the case under the ancient and feudal modes of production. In some situations the dominant social entity might be an economic class more broadly construed, as seen in the domination of the bourgeoisie under the modern capitalist mode of production. Because of this role of organizing the information of a social formation, these societal institutions helped to keep social anarchy and chaos at bay by reflecting the cosmos as seen through the ideological lens of the ruling classes and dominant political factions of the particular society, while working as engines to reproduce this cosmos. The proto-libraries and early libraries collected human knowledge to this end, providing those in positions of power with access to the bodies of knowledge necessary to rule, to the exclusion of those without power, the vast majority of whom were not literate.[17] Finally, the proto-libraries and early libraries

---

17. Edward F. Wente, "The Scribes of Ancient Egypt," in *Civilizations of the Ancient Near East*, vol. IV, ed. Jack M. Sasson (New York: Charles Scribner's Sons, 1995), 2214, wrote that for ancient Egypt it "has been estimated,

contributed to the process of knowledge creation necessary to further the aims of these ruling classes by helping them to cement and maintain power, while using hierarchical and patriarchal political systems, as well as ideology and violence, to exclude those in other class positions. The Great Library of Assurbanipal, built in Nineveh by the king of Assyria in the seventh century BCE, is possibly the most renowned example of a monarchically controlled Bronze Age proto-library. With Assurbanipal's Library, the lines of power were apparent. The Library was the property of Assurbanipal himself and was meant to maintain the welfare of a king who essentially personified the state. By his authority, the Library extended a hierarchical bureaucratic structure that was administered by scribes who were, as Oppenheim wrote, "mentioned among the top administrative officials in Middle Assyrian and Neo-Assyrian texts."[18] Because a significant bulk of the society's information was created and stored in the Library, a large quantity of information was alienated from a majority of the Assyrian people, a people who, I suspect, were to a large degree aware of this alienation.

Since their beginnings, the proto-libraries and early libraries both hoarded and produced knowledge that fell strictly within class boundaries and domination. The earliest known proto-libraries of ancient Mesopotamia have been dated to around 3000 BCE, with a large cache of clay tablets found at the site of the Red Temple at Erech dating to this period.[19] The earliest known Egyptian proto-libraries date to approximately the same time, although there is much less archaeological evidence due to the fact that the Egyptian scribes wrote on papyrus scrolls instead of clay tablets.[20] The Minoan and Mycenaean proto-libraries originated somewhat later than the Mesopotamian and Egyptian

---

primarily on the basis of Old Kingdom evidence, that the literacy rate was about 1 percent overall."

18. A. Leo Oppenheim, *Ancient Mesopotamia: Portrait of a Dead Civilization* (Chicago, IL: University of Chicago Press, 1964), 242-243.

19. Michael H. Harris, *History of Libraries in the Western World*, compact textbook ed. (Metuchen, NJ: Scarecrow Press, 1984), 18.

20. Ibid., 27-28.

institutions, with surviving clay tablets dated from 1900 to 1450 BCE (the Minoan period) and from 1450 to mid-thirteenth century BCE (the Mycenaean period).[21] All of these proto-libraries clearly displayed their political and ideological connections in terms of their ownership and use by rulers and elites.

It is not particularly surprising to learn that the available evidence suggests that written communication developed from early accounting techniques for conducting business transactions. Among the earliest precursors to writing are Mesopotamian symbolic tokens used in trade, and later the clay "egg tablets" designed to hold these transaction tokens.[22] The vast majority of Bronze Age documents that have survived consist of business contracts and sales receipts. The oldest actual written documents are of this type and have been dated to approximately 3000 BCE.[23] So, throughout the history of ancient Mesopotamia and across a variety of the region's great civilizations (Sumerian, Akkadian, Babylonian, Assyrian, etc.), many of the proto-libraries served a function as business archives run by priests, thus blurring the boundaries between the spiritual and economic. In addition to ensuring the continuity of society through the obsessive keeping of business records, all three of the major Bronze Age cultures—Mesopotamian, Egyptian, and Greek—used the proto-libraries to secure their bureaucracies by storing governmental administrative documents.

The proto-libraries of the later Hellenic world were also tightly integrated into the ruling power structure, operating as both bureaucratic instruments and symbols of power. There were also an increasingly large number of privately held libraries due to the invention of the alphabet

---

21. Konstantinos Sp. Staikos, *The History of the Library in Western Civilization*, Vol 1: *From Minos to Cleopatra*, trans. Timothy Cullen (New Castle, DE: Oak Knoll Press, 2004), 12-20.

22. See Denise Schmandt-Besserat, "The Earliest Precursor of Writing," *Scientific American* 238, no. 6 (June 1977), 50-58.

23. Felix Reichmann, *The Sources of Western Literacy: The Middle Eastern Civilizations* (Westport, CT: Greenwood Press, 1980), 22; Samuel Noah Kramer, *History Begins at Sumer: Thirty-Nine Firsts in Man's Recorded History*, 3rd ed. (Philadelphia: University of Pennsylvania Press, 1981), 3.

and increasing literacy rates. Hegemonic power, nonetheless, remained a major motive for collecting books for both state and private proto-libraries. Hoepner wrote that "all or most fourth century [Mediterranean] kings and rulers collected books for prestige reasons,"[24] and that "it was typical of the pre-Hellenistic age for kings and rulers from peripheral areas to commit themselves without reservation to Greek culture." The rulers did this to benefit politically from culturally identifying with the dominant power of the age. If the Hellenic institutions were public (i.e., they belonged to the polis, of which actual citizens were in a minority), they were typically housed in temples. There was a library on the Acropolis, for example, that housed the archives of the city state.[25]

The Great Library of Alexandria, founded ca. 300 BCE by the Greek pharaoh Ptolemy I Soter (lived ca. 367-283 BCE), has the most authentic claim to being the first true academic research library and is a primary candidate for the paradigm of all those academic libraries that came in its wake. But, as with its predecessors, the Great Library was also an important instrument for cementing the hegemony of the ruling class, both in terms of the political authority of the Ptolemaic pharaohs and the cultural supremacy of Egypt's Greek conquerors. This objective, to employ the Great Library as a tool for political and cultural control, was a political maneuver on the part of Ptolemy I. The Pharaoh adopted the tradition of his Egyptian predecessors of building great monuments to display his political power. The Great Lighthouse of Pharos in the port of Alexandria is another example, as is the Museum of Alexandria in the city's Greek quarter, to which the Great Library was attached. The collections at the Museum and Great Library also reflect their use as tools of political and sociocultural hegemony. Erskine wrote that they served an ideological function that encompassed both cultural maintenance and the reproduction of power structures:

---

24. Wolfram Hoepfner, *On Greek Libraries and Bookcases* (Berlin: de Gruyter, 1996), 6.

25. Staikos, *History of the Library in Western Civilization*, vol. 1, 76.

> So the Ptolemaic kingdom may appear abruptly in Egypt without roots, but the Museum and Library link the new kingdom and its Greek inhabitants to Alexander and to a Greek past and present. It is because they help to supply this need that they survive and strengthen. And the more they survive the more they themselves act not as links with a tradition but as the tradition itself. Consequently these institutions can gain still more strength.[26]

Innis described this uptick in cultural activity of societies as "an index of power. A concern for continuity, the biological limitations of the patriarchal system as a basis for dynasties, and the difficulties of maintaining a high cultural level over a long period of time will involve an emphasis on types of architecture calculated to reflect a control over time as well as over space."[27] Every attempt was made by the ruling Greeks to amass the extant Greek literature—at that time the dominant canon of literature—from across the world. The Greek Egyptian rulers also attracted the best academics from across the Hellenic world to engage in large scale scholarly projects, including the translation of non-Greek texts into Greek.[28] The first major scholarly endeavor of the Great Library's scholars was chauvinistic: the rulers of Egypt sought to fix the canon of Greek literature.

All of these ancient civilizations used proto-libraries or early libraries to support what Innis called "oligopolies of knowledge." Oligopolies of knowledge are dialectical constructs that enforce hierarchies of control yet contain the seed of these hegemonies' own destruction:

---

26. Andrew Erskine, "Culture and Power in Ptolemaic Egypt: The Museum and Library of Alexandria," *Greece & Rome*, 2nd Ser., 42, no. 1 (April 1995), 42.

27. Harold A Innis, *The Bias of Communication* (Toronto: University of Toronto Press, 1951), 133.

28. Ptolemy II (lived 309-246 BCE), for instance, imported Jewish scholars to Alexandria to translate the Pentateuch into Greek. Collins wrote that this "would fulfill two objectives in one. Not only would Ptolemy add to his books, but scholars who were experts in Hebrew and Greek would be brought into the city, where the king could tempt them to stay at his court. This would establish Alexandria and its library as a centre of learning, which would reflect the glory of Ptolemy II. See Nina Collins, *The Library in Alexandria and the Bible in Greek* (Leiden: Brill, 2000), 2.

An oral tradition implies freshness and elasticity but students of anthropology have pointed to the binding character of custom in primitive cultures. A complex system of writing becomes the possession of a special class and tends to support aristocracies. A simple flexible system of writing admits of adaptation to the vernacular but slowness of adaptation facilitates monopolies of knowledge and hierarchies. Reading in contrast with writing implies a passive recognition of the power of writing. Inventions in communication compel realignments in the monopoly or the oligarchy of knowledge.[29]

The position of the librarian within such oligopolies has been fetishized since ancient times, supporting the structure. One striking example of the mythologization of the librarian is the case of the "cynocephalus ape" (dog-headed ape or yellow baboon) in ancient Egyptian mythology. Richardson wrote that these apes were the servants of Thoth, the Egyptian god of writing and libraries, and were "sublibrarians" and the patrons of literature, science, and the arts.[30] The cynocephalus ape, Richardson wrote, was seen by the Egyptians as representing writing and equilibrium; they "sit upon the prow of the barque of Ra and live upon truth [...] Passing thus, strictly according to the manner of modern evolution, from the gods upward to man, by way of the ape, we come to the human librarians."[31] Although academic librarians might not like being compared to dog-headed apes, this mythology shows an idealization of their roles in term of wealth, status, and power. If Thoth is a fetishization of knowledge, then his sub-librarians are the administrators of this power. The elevated position of the librarian is found not only in mythological narratives, but in lived history. Because they were among the few literate members of the population and because of their proximity to the political rulers, scribes held powerful positions in these ancient societies. Richardson attested to this elevated position when he noted that one Egyptian scribe was even wealthy enough to own

---

29. Innis, *Bias of Communication*, 4.

30. Ernest Cushing Richardson, *Some Old Egyptian Librarians* (Berkeley, CA: Peacock Press, 1964), 19-20.

31. Ibid., 22.

his own horse.[32] An ancient source from Pharaonic Egypt praises the "blithesome" scribal profession and the benefits that it entails,[33] for the "scribe directs the work of all men. For him there are no taxes, for he pays tribute in writing and there are no dues for him."[34] Such temporal control was jealously guarded. Oppenheim referred to the "stream of tradition," i.e., the function of the Mesopotamian proto-libraries and the scribes as a means of sustaining the traditions of a particular civilization. The literary texts, of which there were not a great number, were kept by the proto-libraries in order to continue the "stream of tradition,"[35] in the process maintaining the scribal classes' hold on power.

The collapse of the gatekeepers' hold on power is tied to the destruction of their control of the ideological superstructures of the societies themselves. This transition of power might result from a transmission of institutional control from one dominating civilization to another, as was the case in the transmission of control of the Great Library between the Hellenistic kingdoms and Rome. Such a transition might, however, result in the complete destruction of the ideological institutions. In fact, the destruction of libraries seems to recur quite frequently in history. Battles noted several reasons for this: as a means of suppression and control by controlling and revising intellectual resources, as sacramental burnings meant for purifying the dominant religion of unauthoritative texts, and as a way to remove undesirable "authors and readers" from history.[36] All of these motives relate back to controlling ideology for the purpose of imposing hegemony.

I will leave this brief history of the ideological library here. If one were to explore the history of the medieval monastic, Byzantine, and Arab libraries, they would find similar basic ideological functions to

---

32. Ibid., 3.

33. Reichmann, *Sources of Western Literacy*, 88.

34. Ibid.

35. A. Leo Oppenheim, "Assyriology—Why and How?" *Current Anthropology* 1, nos. 5-6 (1960): 410.

36. Mathew Battles, *Library: An Unquiet History* (New York: W.W. Norton, 2003), 42.

those existing in the preceding proto-libraries and early libraries. The remainder of this chapter argues that the MCAL supports an oligopoly of knowledge and is an ideological state apparatus that is tasked with minimizing efforts to transform society's fundamental structures.

The MCAL as a Robust Ideological Engine

The recent rapid advances in information technology have resulted in fantastic changes to the library's cosmetic appearance and means and formats of information delivery. Take for instance San Antonio's "library without books," where the stacks are replaced by banks of networked computer terminals.[37] But seemingly in defiance of modernization, not much has changed concerning the MCAL's ideological function in capitalist social formations. This key function, scaffolding the status quo, has remained essentially the same for thousands of years.

At first blush there appears to be little danger in mythologizing the MCAL. Libraries certainly seem like worthy objects to lionize and make eternal, since they remain a primary motivating force behind science, the humanities, education, and human progress in general. Shouldn't the library be revered as an institution? The short answer is yes. We must continue to place great value in our academic libraries or we risk debasing them and losing sight of their missions. But it is important to question mythic narratives in connections to human institutions. Žižek wrote that in *The Prison* Kafka conceptualizes bureaucracy as a proxy for God.[38] Like God, modern bureaucracy and the institutions of state have become the "Big Other," the thing we use to define ourselves. If we once saw ourselves in God, we now impose our characteristics in our modern institutions and then, in essence, receive them back desultorily from those same institutions, perpetuating a cycle of alienation. Academic libraries, therefore, should be approached critically if one wants

---

37. Bill Chappell, "Bookless Public library Opens in Texas," *The Two-Way* (blog), September 14, 2013, http://www.npr.org/blogs/thetwo-way/2013/09/14/222442870/bookless-public-library-opens-in-texas.

38. Slavoj Žižek, *Parallax View* (Cambridge, MA: MIT Press, 2006), 115-116.

to interrupt this cycle. They should be considered historically and not left as inviolate ideas or as accomplices to other seemingly inviolate ideas or institutions like capitalism or social democratic governments. Complacent approaches to history, particularly if these approaches are held by people in positions of influence or power (and, even though they might contest the notion, modern librarians still possess influence and power as information gatekeepers), reproduce the mythic narratives that cloak power relations.

As described previously, there is a mythology surrounding libraries that has been built on political, religious, and philosophical foundations stretching back to the ancient civilizations. Libraries continue to reflect a mythological narrative that evolves with the social formation, even though many of the institution's basic ideas remain sublimated. Maxwell, for instance, noted that throughout history heaven has been used as a metaphor for libraries.[39] In modernity, variations of this heavenly symbolism persist, even if, in some instances, they have been re-inscribed with modernist monikers. Witness the library's identification with Human Potentiality which, although it is derived from ancient religious and philosophical bases, has been repurposed to project the MCAL in a sort of moderno-capitalist utopian light. Wisner described the popular modern view of the library as "the library transformed! Infinite access. A beacon of democratic hope. Seemingly endless possibilities for the advancement of learning, such as to make Francis Bacon himself set sail again from the New Atlantis."[40] Ideas like these suggest that popular perception of the library constructs it as an institution that sits at the juncture of the traditional past, the innovative present, and the utopian future. This popular perception of the library inspires an Ezra Pound-like "Make it new!" optimism at the same time that it continues to be subliminally defined by tradition. This is not an unusual way to think

---

39. Nancy Kalikow Maxwell, *Sacred Stacks: The Higher Purpose of Libraries and Librarianship* (Chicago, IL: American Library Association, 2006), 2.

40. William H. Wisner, *Whither the Postmodern Library? Libraries, Technology, and Education in the Information Age* (Jefferson, NC: McFarland & Company, 1999), 48.

about the MCAL. The capitalist social form is based on and persists because of this convergence of ideas regarding a ceaseless positive expansion reinforced by some underlying mythical idealist permanency. The volume of eulogistic rhetoric concerning libraries suggests that people connect the institution with progress in a way that puts them squarely in line with this dominant capitalist ideology. The success of the capitalist social formation, in fact, shows that it is the latest success of dialectical historical processes, a synthesis that purged the dross from feudalism while maintaining those elements that work well in the new order.

Myth, according to Campbell, serves four functions: mystical, cosmological, sociological, and pedagogical. The mystical function provides signposts pointing towards "the mystery that underlies all forms,"[41] the cosmological function allows humans to map and navigate the world through defining its shape, the sociological function supports the ways in which humans order their realities and situate themselves within this order, and the pedagogical function is the way in which myth operates as a tool to transmit culture and ideology, the means to "live a human lifetime under any circumstances."[42] Libraries past and present are laden with a mythology that has been built up over centuries. Even if much of this mythology is not readily apparent, it informs our primary total ideology or Weltanschauung. It does this, furthermore, in a manner that is beneficial to the predominating social formation by (mythically) ordering and validating one's existence in a stable structural sense, and (again mythically) insuring the continuity of this cosmic structure. In the process, we lose sight of the historical bedrock that comprises much of who we are today. By understanding the mythology of the library as an ideological inheritance, we may then become able to subvert it.

---

41. Joseph Campbell and Bill Moyers, *The Power of Myth* (New York: Doubleday, 1988), 31.

42. Ibid.

In his classic essay "Contradiction and Overdetermination,"[43] Althusser gave an explanation of ideology that collapses the Marxist economic substructure with the societal superstructure (e.g., the political establishment, religion, education, and hence the academic library).[44] Earlier, I described how there is a division in orthodox Marxist theory between the economic base and the so-called elements of the superstructure, e.g., the government, the military, and the educational system. These institutions and social phenomena are understood to have arisen out of and to reflect the economic base. This theory, while important in that it looks for explanations for phenomena within the deeper matrix of human social relations, has led to accusations of economic reductionism and vulgar determinism. Although the dualistic understanding of the base/superstructure dichotomy was most likely not the intention of either Marx or Engels, by the end of the nineteenth century, between Marx's death and the early years of the Soviet Union, the conceptual opposition between base and superstructure became codified and dogmatic. However, with his development of the theories of overdetermination and ideological state apparatuses (ISAs), Althusser provided a sophisticated explanation of the base/superstructure relationship that integrated the base and superstructure into one another and identified a possible mechanism for the persistence of the dominant mode of production.

Althusser transformed Freudian overdetermination into a sociological explanation for the reproduction of social formations. While Freud theorized that elements of the subconscious, such as dreams, are the result of multiple causations and cannot be reduced to a single source

---

43. Louis Althusser, "Contradiction and Overdetermination: Notes for an Investigation," in *For Marx*, trans. Ben Brewster, pp. 87-128 (London: Penguin Press, 1965).

44. While Althusser has been accused of rejecting dialectic, he in fact maintained and deepened dialectics by recognizing the multiplicities of determinations involved in the composition of reality (as opposed to the solely economic determination as held by many orthodox Marxists), the fluid network of relationships between phenomena that essentially integrate the economic base with the superstructure and the elements of the superstructure with each other, as well as the relative autonomy of these elements.

or event, Althusser adapted overdetermination to dismiss the dogmatic base/superstructure split in favor of an explanation of sociocultural production that was multi-causal and only traceable to economics in "the last instance,"[45] an instance which never actually comes. Although this was an apparently bold departure from orthodoxy, Althusser grounded his analysis in classical Marxism by tracing his overdetermination to an 1894 letter that Engels wrote to Starkenburg, where Engels opined that the "political, juridical, philosophical, religious, literary, artistic, etc., development is based on economic development. But all these react upon one another and also upon the economic base."[46] By acknowledging the complexity of sociocultural reproduction, as well as the contribution of the multitude of discrete parts of the superstructure in codetermining the nature of the objective whole through a network of relations, Althusser identified the conservative power of human institutions as ideological scaffolding, making institutions like the Church more than just reflections of a civilization's economic underpinnings. Instead, sociocultural institutions vented the tension caused by societal contradictions, acting as a check against dialectical movement and progressive change. These sociocultural institutions, therefore, are at least in part responsible for supporting the social environment and the tenacious constancy of class structures within societies.

In combination with his overdetermination, Althusser's theory of ideological state apparatuses (ISAs) allows the critical analyst to locate the MCAL as a component of the societal superstructure responsible for cultivating the status quo. For the time being, let us concentrate on the role of the MCAL as an ideological institution in fixing the best interests of the dominant class as the status quo, thus hampering dialectical change.

---

45. Louis Althusser, "Contradiction and Overdetermination: Notes for an Investigation," in *For Marx*, translated by Ben Brewster (London: Penguin Press, 1965), 111.

46. Karl Marx and Friedrich Engels, *Selected Correspondence 1846-1889 with Commentary and Notes*, trans. Dona Torr (London: Lawrence & Wishart, 1936), 517.

Althusser wrote:

> I shall say that the reproduction of labour power requires not only a reproduction of its skills, but also, at the same time, a reproduction of its submission to the rules of the established order, i.e. a reproduction of submission to the ruling ideology for the workers, and a reproduction of the ability to manipulate the ruling ideology correctly for the agents of exploitation and repression, so that they too, will provide for the domination of the ruling class 'in word'.[47]

Raber applied Althusser's theory of ideology to the American public library and determined it to be an ISA because it is state-maintained and elicits people's consent to hegemony.[48] This same description applies to the MCAL. Budd wrote that librarians need to "overcome a conservatism (not in the party-political sense) that preserves past action and thought as inherently good and useful."[49] The MCAL as an ISA makes use of this conservatism to perpetuate the dominant ideological view of them as "good and useful."

As an ISA, the MCAL performs this function in a (seemingly) benign way, as opposed to "violence,"[50] that is, the oftentimes outright administrative or physical coercion used by societal institutions like the judicial system and military and police forces, what Althusser called the repressive state apparatuses (RSAs). The ISAs, instead, rely primarily on the primacy of the "word."[51] What Althusser means by this "silent" influence by the "word" is that the ISAs reinforce (and oftentimes do so implicitly) the established rules of comportment within the socio-cultural milieu.

---

47. Louis Althusser, "Ideology and the Ideological State Apparatuses," in *Lenin and Philosophy and Other Essays*, trans. Ben Brewster (New York: Monthly Review Press, 2001), 89.

48. Douglas Raber, "Librarians as Organic Intellectuals: A Gramscian Approach to Blind Spots and Tunnel Vision." *Library Quarterly* 68, no. 1 (2003): 49.

49. John M. Budd, *Self-Examination: The Present and Future of Librarianship* (Westport, CT: Libraries Unlimited, 2008), 226.

50. Althusser, "Ideology and the Ideological State Apparatuses," 97.

51. Ibid., 93.

The ISAs manufacture acceptance—whether it be cheerful, grudging, or indifferent—towards the existing power relations through teaching the "rules of good behavior" and ultimately "the rules of the order established by class domination."[52] Essentially this process reproduces what Gramsci called the hegemony of the "dominant fundamental group."[53] Exploitation is transformed into a constant; it is mythologized and normalized. In the process, the dehumanizing relations of capitalism are hidden by an ideological curtain based on idealism. The major advantage of this ideological support for the status quo is that it avoids social turmoil, even if this avoidance comes at the expense of marginalized groups. A social formation without ideological scaffolding, if it were even possible, would devolve into utter chaos. The concern with the ISAs under capitalism, however, is that if, as Marx and Althusser contended, the state represents the interests of the dominant class, the capitalist ISAs function ultimately inhibits the development of human freedom of all people, and particularly the freedom of the subaltern classes.

Althusser listed several modern ISAs existing under capitalism including the "Religious ISA (the system of different Churches), the educational ISA, the family ISA, the legal ISA, the political ISA (the political system, including the different parties), the trade union ISA, the communications ISA, [and] the cultural ISA (Literature, the Arts, sports, etc.)."[54] Dietzgen's dialectics has similarities with Althusser's concept of overdetermination, presaging Althusser's ideas concerning the material realization of ideology. Similar to Dietzgen's understanding of materialism, all of Althusser's ISAs are materially realized networks of actions and ideas. They interact dialectically with human beings that, in turn, may only be adequately defined in terms of their material relationships with these institutions:

---

52. Ibid.

53. Antonio Gramsci, *Selections from the Prison Notebooks*, ed. and trans. Quinton Hoare and Geoffrey Nowell Smith (New York: International Publishers, 1971), 12.

54. Althusser, "Ideology and the Ideological State Apparatuses," 96.

> The individual in question behaves in such and such a way, adopts such and such a practical attitude, and, what is more, participates in certain regular practices which are those of the ideological apparatus on which 'depend' the ideas which he has in all consciousness freely chosen as a subject. If he believes in God, he goes to Church to attend Mass, kneels, prays, confesses, does penance (once it was material in the ordinary sense of the term) and naturally represents and so on.[55]

Ideology, according to this conceptualization, is materially constituted through this interaction. By acknowledging the complexity of reality, Althusser's overdetermination recovered a materialism that had essentially become dualistic and reductive. Compare Althusser's concept of overdetermination with Dietzgen's conclusion that:

> Reason is a real thing only in so far as it is perceived by the senses. The perceptible actions of reason are revealed in the brain of man as well as in the world outside of it. For are not the effects tangible by which reason transforms nature and life? […] If we wish to regard the world in the light of the "thing itself," we shall easily see that the world "itself" and the world as it appears, the world of phenomena, differ only in the same way in which the whole differs from its component parts. The world "itself" is nothing else but the sum total of its phenomena. The same holds good of that part of the world that we call reason, spirit, faculty of thought.[56]

In effect, this viewpoint, one which allows for ideologies (e.g., library philosophy) to be understood as just as material in nature as things like physical edifices (e.g., the library building), integrates the economic base, which is traditionally seen as the generative substructure by Marxists, with the societal superstructure. It allows institutions like the academic library, as ISAs, to be seen as both loci of change and the terrain of class struggle.

---

55. Ibid., 113.

56. Joseph Dietzgen. *The Nature of Human Brainwork: An Introduction to Dialectics* (Oakland, PA: PM Press 2010), 28-29.

What is the primary function of the MCAL in terms of ideology and sociocultural conservatorship? As with their historical predecessors, they support the political/economic status quo and they actively create history bound within the ideological restrictions imposed by the prevailing mode of production. The MCAL is particularly effective at this task because not only is it an educational ISA, which Althusser identified as the dominant Ideological State Apparatus of capitalism,[57] but it also contains elements and functions of three other capitalist ISAs: the communications ISA, the cultural ISA, and the religious ISA.

Applying Althusser to the MCAL, one can see that if the fundamental ideological facet of capitalism is embodied by the educational system, a dominant position that education has taken over from religion, the MCAL is also fundamental to reproducing capitalism. Freire wrote that the "educated man is the adapted man because he is better 'fit' for the world."[58] The capitalist educational system "fits" students, and sensibly so when considering basic self-preservation of the social structure, for a capitalist world. The MCAL is the center of academic knowledge on the college campus, serving as the central repository for the ideas disseminated, investigated, and reproduced at the college or university. The very fact that an item is included in a library collection (either physically or electronically), and that it is organized and retrieved by trained academic librarians, lends the MCAL credibility and authority. As a node of the communications ISA, the obvious operation of the MCAL is to act as a mechanism for disseminating information. The library is a hub for scholarly communication and research dissemination, as well as an outlet for news and trade publications. As a cultural ISA, the MCAL is a reservoir for both popular and high culture. A library's collection both generates culture with the products emerging from its use, and is a conduit for making culture available to its publics through things like library programming. Finally, as a (crypto) religious ISA, the MCAL continues

---

57. Althusser, "Ideology and the Ideological State Apparatuses," 103.

58. Paulo Freire, *Pedagogy of the Oppressed*, trans. Myra Bergman Ramos (New York: Continuum, 1970), 63.

to implicitly fashion people's relationship to capitalism. According to Althusser, the religious ISA—embodied materially and socially by the Church—was the primary pre-capitalist ISA, prior to the educational ISA ascending to the position under capitalism.[59] For most of its history, academic libraries were temples, and their librarians were priests. Although capitalism has been accompanied by an increase in secularism, with the majority of academic libraries being ostensibly secular, these same institutions incorporate elements of the religious ISA, acting as "crypto-temples."[60] For example, libraries tend to be geographically centered on campus, bear elements of Eliade's understanding of temples as "cosmic mountains,"[61] and implement a hierarchical organization both in their ordering of the universe of knowledge as well as in their internal administrative organization. This religious presence, although it is somewhat sublimated, imposes patriarchal ideologies—also associated with capitalist society—on its users through orienting those that come into contact with it as "supplicants."[62]

In its capacity as an ISA, the MCAL is a coadjutor to neoliberal capitalism. It is particularly effective at institutionalizing stasis because it strongly incorporates many other ISAs.

Introducing Counter-Hegemony as an Alternative

Academic libraries, nonetheless, are by no means monolithic in terms of ideology. The MCALs are hotbeds for the production of ideologies, both ideologies as narrowly construed (i.e., as a personally held credo), and as *Weltanschauung* (i.e., as an overarching framework such as

---

59. Althusser, "Ideology and the Ideological State Apparatuses," 102.

60. Stephen Bales, "Academic Library as Crypto-Temple," *Class and Librarianship: Essays at the Intersection of Information, Labor and Capital*, eds. Erik Estep and Nathaniel Enright (Sacramento, CA: Library Juice Press, forthcoming).

61. Mircea Eliade, *The Sacred and the Profane: The Nature of Religion*, trans. William A. Trask (New York: Harcourt Brace, 1987), 39.

62. Bales, "Capitalist Academic Library as a Crypto-Temple: A Marxian Analysis," forthcoming.

capitalism or socialism). As a material force, the MCAL encapsulates both of these types of ideologies. For example, an academic librarian may subscribe to the tenets of dialectical materialism in the ideological sense, or be an avowed capitalist, and a patron may subscribe to a conservative viewpoint that reflects in their particular use of the library. This tangle of ideologies, furthermore, is itself dialectical; individual credos come into conflict with each other and the broader function of the MCAL as a capitalist apparatus. Even though the MCAL is a capitalist apparatus, it fosters counter-hegemony. Despite their status as ISAs, it is apparent throughout the history of academic libraries that, in spite of their conservative functions, they have born a measure of responsibility for the transition from one historical social formation to the next, whether this transition is through gradual change or through rapid, violent revolution. For instance, the collapse of the Roman Empire and the shift from ancient to feudal social structures has been attributed to many different factors. Rome's downfall has been connected with disparate phenomena, such as the rise of Christianity, rampant inflation, the "barbarianization" of the Roman army, and even lead poisoning. If one views the fall from an Althusserian perspective, it seems more likely that some (ultimately dialectical!) combination of these and other factors resulted in the relatively abrupt and violent revolution in structure, and it is plausible that the various library catastrophes, such as the multiple burnings of the Great Library of Alexandria or possibly even the murder of the late antique philosopher/librarian Hypatia, played some part in ushering in the radical transformation. Not only is change to the status quo often accompanied by the destruction of libraries, libraries themselves have served counter-hegemonic functions, incubating the development of controversial and confrontational ideas and actions. Marx, for instance, extensively used the British Museum, a symbol of the temporal hegemony of the most industrialized nation of the time period, to write *Capital*, his most revolutionary work.

The MCAL, therefore, is not simply an engine for reproducing dominant ideologies, but it may also act as a place for creating, housing, and transmitting counter-hegemony, even if its stereotypes of solitude and quiet belie this conflict. Understanding the ideological nature of the MCAL leads the critical analyst to the necessary conclusion that the ISA is not the only material expression possible for modern libraries, and that it is possible to develop alternative, counter-hegemonic ideological expressions. Various Italian anarchist libraries, for instance, have operated in the twentieth and twenty-first centuries.[63] The NYC Occupy Wall Street movement of 2011 inspired the creation of social justice oriented support library services including a myMETROresearchers project which partnered with Occupy to provide free research support for Occupy activists,[64] and the "People's Library," a free library serving NYC Occupy that actively sought to subvert traditional institutional power relations:

> The Library Working Group works on consensus. When I was in library school, we talked about horizontal structures and consensus as a cutting edge way of organizing library work and staff. Please throw that all out the window. Please. The meaning of "consensus" used in my library school classroom and the meaning of it at the Occupation and in radical politics generally are not the same. For us, consensus requires that nearly everyone support a decision. If there are people with serious concerns about a proposal, what we call a "block," we need at least 90% those present to be in support of it. Degreed librarians have no more weight in making decisions than an 18-year-old college student, an underemployed actress, or a crusty traveling kid.[65]

These exceptions to hegemony are distinguished by the fact that their political intentions are clearly manifest through public political and social

---

63. See Luigi Balsamini, "Libraries and Archives of the Anarchist Movement in Italy," *Progressive Librarian*, no. 40 (Fall/Winter 2012), 1-15.

64. Darcy Gervasio, Angela Ecklund, and Arieh Ross, "Library Research for the 99%: Reaching Out to the Occupy Wall Street Movement," *Urban Library Journal* 19, no. 1 (2013), http://ojs.gc.cuny.edu/index.php/urbanlibrary/article/view/1398/pdf_10.

65. Daniel Norton, Mandy Henk, Betsy Fagin, Jaime Taylor, and Zachary Loeb, "Occupy Wall Street Librarians Speak Out," *Progressive Librarian* nos. 38/39 (2012): 6.

platforms and agendas. While these libraries and archives may claim some measure of success, they represent encouraging but ultimately marginal cases. What can we do at the MCALs to move them towards counter-hegemony?

The MCAL is, at its root, a conservative institution that resists the elemental and progressive changes associated with dialectical motion, largely because such changes are not often in the interest of the predominant, and exploitative, social class, a class that ultimately owns and jealously guards the means of production. This idea is disconcerting, especially to the large portion of a society that accepts the myths that the MCAL is an inherently benevolent and politically neutral institution and that academic librarianship is a politically neutral profession. But, if we critique the Big Ideas of the academic library, inevitably we start to see past them. Parsing the threads of the past, present, and future MCAL becomes a key feature of the critical analysis of the institution and of us. Furthermore, concrete material contextualization allows the analyst to project her analysis forward to forecast the MCAL's probable futures.[66] An understanding of the range of probable futures, coupled with the knowledge of how dialectical movement occurs within historical context, supports the analyst in her capacity as a change agent; she knows what to aim at and has effective weapons to hit her target.

Such an orientation carries with it profound implications for the theoretically conscious academic librarian. Once making the commitment to engage in theoretically informed and guided praxis, the critical analyst may no longer accept surface phenomena *de facto*. She no longer, so to speak, flies blind. Instead, she now uses observation, reason, and her understanding of history and the basic dialectical principles to gain insight into the deeper meanings and relationships that are obscured by surface phenomena. In turn, this approach to understanding allows her to refine her own ideology in the face of her deeply contemplated practical experiences. That is, the theoretically conscious academic librarian

---

66. Bertell Ollman, *Dance of the Dialectic: Steps in Marx's Method* (Urbana, IL: University of Illinois Press, 2003), 167-168.

becomes consciously aware that she can continue to refine her ideological standpoint through transformative praxis until it best conforms to her critically derived understanding of the world. She then works to conform the MCAL to this same standpoint. The critical analyst knows that, as an historical actor, she may either serve as an agent of the status quo or as a change agent, and that ideology, as a historical phenomenon, may be affected by her as part of the dialectical process. Therefore, whatever path the librarian chooses to take, the academic librarian is never an apolitical subject. In chapter 5, I address this idea of counter-hegemonic change by further outlining a case for the professional academic librarians who work in an institution with which they are, at a fundamental level, ideologically opposed, and who do this for the purpose of affecting an elemental ideological transformation upon the MCAL itself.

Chapter 5

THE COUNTER-HEGEMONIC ACADEMIC LIBRARIAN

Everybody is to some degree aware of the inevitability of social change, even if many people do not routinely consider such change in any dialectical sense. Because of this basic understanding of their reality, humans have both consciously (e.g., by means of policy and procedure) and unconsciously (e.g., by immersion in a *Weltanschauung*) erected social apparatuses to manage this social change. These ISAs may result in both positive and negative outcomes. For instance, although the academic library quite effectively and dramatically supports both the preservation and advancement of knowledge, and has done so by maintaining certain principles and philosophies surrounding its basic missions even in the face of rapid technological advancements, it still operates as a support for a capitalist social formation that is fundamentally exploitative. This is because total ideologies are usually successful ideologies, at least in terms of their ability to survive. They cloak their antagonisms well. Take, for instance, the recent debates in the U.S. over white privilege and the troubling fact that in 2015 large segments of the American public refuse to acknowledge the possibility that it even exists. Because of neoliberal capitalism's effectiveness at appearing to be natural, as well as its impressive ability to reproduce its ideology through capitalist ISAs like the MCAL, it is not surprising that many contradictions are left unconsidered and never acted upon.

Nonetheless, the MCALs employ a large number of potential change agents. Academic librarians are typically optimists and visionaries when it comes to their view of the MCAL. This hopeful farsightedness comes in part because their work at the MCAL lets them simultaneously observe and take part in libraries' rapidly accelerating change, in the process illuminating its potentialities. Their direct interaction with the MCAL also attunes them to areas of deficiency and stagnation that should be addressed to maintain forward momentum. For instance, academic librarians have been on the forefront of issues like the growing digital divide and the looming digital dark age. In addition to their front-line exposure, academic librarians often possess a basic respect for the cultural-historical concepts attached to the MCAL. Unfortunately, idealism is counterproductive when the source of the idealism—in this instance the academic library as the embodiment of big, eternal, possibly even God-given ideas—both supports and is braced by a material reality that may run counter to the core values espoused by the idealist. Most academic librarians realize that contradictions exist where they work, and with observation and introspection (and after a lot of reading), dissatisfaction with the MCAL may lead the academic librarian to assume a progressive, counter-hegemonic praxis.[1]

Intellectuals who understand the material nature of reality are well-positioned to offer social critique of the institutions at which they work. Unfortunately, academics who resist or refute ideological structures enforced and reproduced by the ISAs are often labeled as eccentric, deviant, or sometimes even treasonous. This stigmatization has done much to strip social science discourse and research of its potentially transformative political elements. That is, the conservative drive to maintain the status quo has led to the scholasticization of critical discourse. This conservative drive has silenced critique through the marginalization of critical methods in LIS graduate school, and more overtly through influencing hiring and tenure practices.

---

1. An initial task for the counter-hegemonic academic librarian, even if she has not yet delved into the intricacies of materialist dialectics, is to expand her critical consciousness concerning the dominant culture's reliance on abstraction as a means of hegemonic control; this allows her to better understand what these simplistic abstractions mean in the context of their daily work lives. It allows her to locate the abstracted concepts in situ and to map their relationships with capitalism's other phenomena.

But if one accepts that the positions that I have put forward concerning the MCAL as an ideological institution are correct, i.e., that academic libraries are ISAs tasked with maintaining and reproducing the dominant ideologies of the particular historical social formations in which they operate, and thus maintaining and reproducing the social formations themselves, then one must question the current roles of academic librarians within these ISAs. Chapter 4 introduced the idea of the counter-hegemonic academic librarian as a historically and politically conscious role that the practicing academic librarian may assume in response to the ideological landscape in which they work. This chapter promotes the concept of the counter-hegemonic academic librarian as an important foil to the MCAL as ISA, as an actively engaged, politically oriented conduit for, and generator of, materially realized theory regarding the institution. I posit that academic librarians are already politically aligned, organic intellectuals who, if they have not already, must choose between hegemony and counter-hegemony if they wish to maintain a sense of personal and professional integrity. I conclude with comments on the relationships between academic librarianship, dialectics, and counter-hegemonic praxis.

The Role of the LIS Practitioner in Effecting Socially Progressive Change

Even though the MCAL is a locus for revolutionary impulses, it is both shrouded and restricted by the dominant hegemonic ideologies. The institution has been, is currently, and presumably will remain a powerful cultural and political tool, even if elements of its sociopolitical constitution remain hidden beneath a veneer of professional neutrality. The very concept of neutrality suggests social stasis. Academic librarians must be accounted for as powerful sociocultural and sociopolitical actors, especially when one considers their role within the institutional matrix of the library as information gatekeepers and policymakers. The underlying social function of the academic librarian may be provisionally categorized in a binary manner. First, whether they are aware of it or not, the majority of academic librarians operate as functionaries of the neoliberal state. Nonetheless, in contrast to, but not necessarily in conscious opposition to this group of professionals, exists a smaller category of progressive academic librarians whose members operate at varying levels of political consciousness. The membership of this second category of professionals question the existing sociopolitical structure of society and are not often satisfied with what they find. Because of this disappointment, they seek to understand the MCAL's potential roles in both supporting and subverting this social reality and, ideally, they use this knowledge to work towards realizing meaningful change.

I have argued that human social relations are relative and shifting because of history and circumstance, and that these relations may be consciously reconfigured towards political, social, and economic goals. But why should academic librarians study the power relationships of where they work, and why should they do this for the purpose of effecting strategic change? In the broad professional sense, and despite recurrent pretensions of scientific impartiality, academic librarianship expresses its normative goals in its many published statements on professional principles. For instance, the first article of the Library Bill of Rights of the American Library Association (ALA) lists the "enlightenment of all people of the community the library serves" as a basic policy[2] The first principle of the "Ethical Principles for Library and Information Professionals" of the Chartered Institute of Library and Information Professional's (CILIP) calls for a professional concern for "the public good in all professional matters, including respect for diversity within society, and the promoting of equal opportunities and human rights."[3] It is also fair to assume that most people choose to become academic librarians without prior knowledge of these statements, but that they choose the career path to some degree because academic librarianship is

---

[2]. American Library Association, "Library Bill of Rights," in *Intellectual Freedom Manual*, 8th ed. (Chicago, IL: American Library Association, 2010), 49.

[3]. Chartered Institute of Library and Information Professionals, "Ethical Principles for Library and Information Professionals," accessed August 6, 2014, http://www.cilip.org.uk/cilip/about/ethics/ethical-principles.

a service profession and they are attracted by the aspirations championed in these principles. Critical analysis and progressive praxis are ways to fulfill both these institutional and personal motivators.

Budd wrote that the "essential character of ethics in librarianship includes recognition that, as a profession, the concern is for the public life of participants and their public actions."[4] This is a dialectically rich statement because it invites one to consider both actors and actions in terms of the value of the whole, i.e., the community that is the totality of public actions. As a professional, one who *professes*, the academic librarian professes her belief in both the importance of human history and the desirability of human progress (both of which are collective endeavors), and she works towards preserving and providing access to the former in service of the latter. She believes that the academic library must ultimately benefit the general human welfare through its support of education and research, feels some responsibility for assisting in this mission, and gains satisfaction by working towards these ends. Counter-hegemonic academic librarianship as a professional practice, therefore, is very much a normative undertaking that combines librarianship's intuitive altruism with a reasoned political and theoretical stance. Critical reflection upon the academic library as flux is coupled with a commitment to guide any change that occurs in a direction that hopefully benefits everyone touched by the institution, but particularly those who are marginalized, with the understanding that benefiting those deemed peripheral ultimately benefits all by reconstituting the totality in a positive manner.[5]

I believe that any social theory that is generated apart from the goal of progressive normative change is, at best, intellectually sterile and lifeless. At worst, such a social theory can be dangerous. This is not to say that normative social science cannot also be dangerous; Dick pointed to

---

4. John M. Budd, "Toward a Practical and Normative Ethics for Librarianship," *Library Quarterly* 76, no. 3 (July 2006): 252.

5. And, as I argue in this book, everyone who is influenced by the academic library is, in fact, *everyone that exists* (past, present, and future).

Nazi anthropology as one gross example of such a pitfall.[6] Normative approaches to social theory and practice, however, may be engaged in responsibly if done in a conscious manner in which practitioners, as Paolo Freire wrote, "reexamine themselves constantly."[7] That is, if a critical praxis is to account for the effect of social relations, it must account for the ramifications of the analyst herself *qua* social relation. Finally, it has been compellingly argued in the spate of recent literature concerning the irrationality of concepts like library value neutrality,[8] that a normative approach to librarianship is also an intellectually honest approach to librarianship.

There is also an ongoing debate as to whether Marxist critical analysis is a normative social scientific pursuit, but I believe that much of the resistance to developing a Marxist ethic stems from nineteenth-century efforts to align it with positivist science. Cohen, however, felt that, while Marx purposefully ignored questions of ethics, it was necessary to reconsider the subject. Marxism, he wrote, "set itself the task of liberating humanity from the oppression that the capitalist market visits upon them."[9] Similarly, Harrington concluded that Marx's socialist vision was essentially utopian and hence normative, that

> Marx had to have a notion of what humans should and could become. Men and women were alienated from that futuristic potential—that possibility of "human nature"—that no one had ever seen and that had never existed. It was only in terms of the radical—utopian—notion

---

6. Archie Dick, "Library and Information Science as a Social Science: Neutral and Normative Conceptions," *Library Review* 65, no. 2 (1995): 226.

7. Paulo Freire, *Pedagogy of the Oppressed*, trans. Myra Bergman Ramos (New York: Continuum, 1970), 47.

8. There is a particularly vibrant discussion concerning the topic of library neutrality occurring in the pages of journals such as *Progressive Librarian*, *Information for Social Change*, and *Information, Society and Justice*. For an excellent collection of edited essays that argue for pro-advocatory librarianship, see Alison Lewis, ed. *Questioning Library Neutrality: Essays from Progressive Librarian* (Duluth, MN: Library Juice Press, 2008).

9. G. A. Cohen, *If You're an Egalitarian, How Come You're So Rich?* (Cambridge, MA: Harvard University Press, 2000), 180.

of what people could become that Marx could so clearly define their present degradation."[10]

Marxism questions the unbiased nature of mainstream approaches to science and philosophy and most Marxist thinkers make clear their own political bias in favor of the working and dispossessed classes of society. If one accepts the Marxist view that all science and philosophy is intrinsically political, even if this political orientation may be mystified, then politically conscious Marxist analysts may not be accused of being politically unscrupulous, in contrast to "neutral" academics and professionals who do not own up to their innate political biases. Socially conscious approaches to LIS and Marxist critical analysis, consequently, appear to complement each other. Both aim at increasing the general welfare through direct encounter with the social formation, and the latter works as a theoretical framing device and toolkit for focusing the progressive energy and enthusiasm of the former. Doherty noted that most librarians, unfortunately, are not reflective, that they hide behind concepts like impartiality, and that by doing this they "exempt themselves from the self-reflection necessary to praxis."[11] But again, academic librarians are intimately familiar with change. Exposure to persuasive theory may be an effective way to coax them into reevaluating and challenging their own personal stasis.

The Theoretical Underpinnings of Counter-Hegemonic Librarianship

The conceptual debate over library neutrality, that librarians are obligated to remain impartial as part of their professional duties, is presently being dominated, and I would argue it is being won, by those authors who write in favor of advocatory librarianship. Witness the dearth of

---

10. Michael Harrington, *Socialism: Past and Future* (New York: Arcade Publishing, 1989), 38.

11. John J. Doherty, "Towards Self-Reflection in Librarianship: What is Praxis?" in *Questioning Library Neutrality: Essays from Progressive Librarian*, ed. Alison Lewis (Duluth, MN: Library Juice Press, 2008), 110.

recent scholarly publications in favor of nonpartisan librarianship. Other than opinion pieces and listserv disputes, calls for neutrality, it seems, are beginning to be relegated to the official statements of professional associations, boilerplate lectures in college classrooms, and textbooks, all of which often benefit by avoiding openly stated political positions. In his essay, "The Myth of the Neutral Professional," Jenson dispatches with library neutrality:

> In the political and philosophical sense in which I use the term here, neutrality is impossible. In any situation, there exists a distribution of power. Overtly endorsing or contesting that distribution are, of course, political choices; such positions are not neutral. But to take no explicit position by claiming to be neutral is also a political choice, particularly when one is given the resources that make it easy to evaluate the consequences of that distribution of power and potentially affect its distribution.[12]

Jenson traced this myth of neutrality to the development of modern librarianship itself, which he wrote was molded by business interests,[13] a cause that relies on the perpetuation of concepts like impartiality and non-regulation for its continued survival. Building on the works of LIS social theorists including Harris[14] and Wiegand,[15] Raber argued against even the *possibility* of neutrality by applying Gramsci's concept of "organic intellectuals" to public librarians.[16] Gramsci's development

---

12. Mark Rosenzweig, "Politics and Anti-Politics in Librarianship," in *Questioning Library Neutrality: Essays from Progressive Librarian*, ed. Alison Lewis (Duluth, MN: Library Juice Press, 2008), 5.

13. Robert Jenson, "The Myth of the Neutral Professional," in *Questioning Library Neutrality: Essays from Progressive Librarian*, ed. Alison Lewis (Duluth, MN: Library Juice Press, 2008), 91.

14. Michael H. Harris, "State, Class, and Cultural Reproduction: Toward a Theory of Library Service in the United States," *Advances in Librarianship* 14 (1986): 211-252.

15. Wayne A. Wiegand, "Tunnel Visions and Blind Spots: What the Past tells us about the Present: Reflections on the Twentieth-Century History of American Librarianship," *Library Quarterly* 69, no. 1 (1999): 1-32.

16. Douglas Raber, "Librarians as Organic Intellectuals: A Gramscian Approach to Blind Spots and Tunnel Vision." *Library Quarterly* 68, no. 1

of the concept of hegemony offers an explanation of how societal norms, regardless of whether they are equitable or exploitative, persist because of subaltern groups' passive acceptance of the authority of dominant groups.[17] Since the prevailing social relations are weighted to the advantage of dominant class interests, they support concepts like Equality in what Freire called a "prescriptive" sense, meaning that it is given to the dominated classes by the hegemonic class and represents the hegemonic class's consciousness and view of reality.[18] Both the oppressed and dominated classes, according to Freire, internalize this oppression—they are "domesticated" by it—and do not work consciously towards realizing their own freedom as human beings.[19] The key word here is "consciously," which implies that awareness brings with it a material agency for effecting cultural and political change. Gramsci explored the possibility of counter-hegemonic struggle, particularly in his ideas concerning the role of partisan intellectuals, i.e., the organic intellectuals.[20] According to his *Prison Notebooks*, intellectuals are attached to a particular social class and work towards the interests of that class, whether they do this in a consciously biased way or they do so as "neutral," "traditional [professional] intellectuals" who work ultimately for the dominant class.[21] Raber wrote that "librarians can be viewed as 'organic intellectuals' and that they play an ideological and organizational role in maintaining a historic bloc's hegemony over the relations of economic production and civil society."[22] Applying Raber's theoretical standpoints to academic librarianship, Bales and Engle concluded that responsible "academic librarians must be cognizant and critical of

---

(2003): 33-53.

17. Antonio Gramsci, *Selections from the Prison Notebooks*, ed. and trans. Quinton Hoare and Geoffrey Nowell Smith (New York: International Publishers, 1971), 60.

18. Freire, *Pedagogy of the Oppressed*, 31.

19. Ibid., 36.

20. Gramsci, *Selections from the Prison Notebooks*, 123.

21. Ibid., 60.

22. Douglas Raber, "Librarians as Organic Intellectuals," 35.

ideological influences, understand that they saturate thought and action, and, following necessarily upon this, own and/or disown specific ideological positions."[23] That is, reflection leads academic librarians to the understanding that they are in some capacity organic to a social group, and this realization leaves them with the responsibility to either accept this role or realign themselves to support another group. Assuming a counter-hegemonic position means consciously taking a proactive, pro-dialogic relationship to reality, i.e., purposefully aligning oneself towards the MCAL's aspect of motion and doing this in opposition to its contradictory aspect of stasis.

Dialectical synthesis results in progress because it resolves conflicts between contradictory elements. Emerging counter-hegemonic cultures should be explored and fostered as potential resolutions for the contradictions found in the dominant culture. Even though the ISAs may seem daunting in terms of their monolithic bureaucratic presences, they are also sites of opposition and struggle in which, as Althusser wrote, "the resistance of the exploited classes is able to find means and occasions to express itself [in the ISA], either by the utilization of their contradictions, or by conquering combat positions in them in struggle."[24] According to Aronowitz and Giroux, working in an institution that doubles as an ideological apparatus does not necessarily truncate the professional academic's capacity to effect meaningful change through this institution, to recognize the academic library as a terrain of struggle that involves the conflict of material ideas and physical material, and to transfigure where they work in light of this recognition. This work is performed by "transformative intellectuals," Aronowitz and Giroux's iteration of the Gramscian organic intellectual. The transformative intellectual is a professional educator who engages in social critique and self-criticism in order to lawfully transform the ideological and material conditions

---

23. Stephen E. Bales and Lea Susan Engle, "The Counterhegemonic Academic Librarian: A Call to Action," *Progressive Librarian* 40 (2012), 23.

24. Louis Althusser, "Ideology and Ideological State Apparatuses: Notes towards an Investigation," in *Lenin and Philosophy and Other Essays*, trans. Ben Brewster (New York: Monthly Review Press, 2001), 99.

of the school from the inside.[25] This is a praxis of protracted struggle, a thread in Gramsci's "war of position," the complex political struggle in which "ideas have power, and the progressive material reform of the relations of production that genuinely improve the life outcomes of the oppressed is possible, even though such change may fall short of revolutionary transformation."[26] Counter-hegemonic praxis is a viable option for academic librarians, and is one that, despite the fear generated against it by the ISA, may be practiced effectively within the ISA without the practitioners having to lose their jobs.

Professional Praxis

To fully understand dialectic is to understand the necessity of praxis, the material realization of theory, as a means to engage effectively with material reality. We have seen, as Marx wrote in the "Theses on Feuerbach," that "the philosophers have only interpreted the world in various ways; the point, however, is to change it."[27] Dialectical materialism supports this position, because if mind is considered as being as materially extant as any physical phenomena, and every particular thing is considered as simultaneously containing the whole because of the interrelatedness of all things, then the act of philosophizing affects the constitution of both the totality and every composite part comprising this totality. Academic Marxism, ironically, is an example of the alienation of theory from practice which Godatti described as a distortion, making it "not a revolutionary instrument, but, rather, a conservative

---

25. Stanley Aronowitz and Henry A. Giroux, *Education Still under Seige*, 2nd ed. (Westport, CT: Bergin and Garvey, 1993), 46.

26. Douglas Raber, "Hegemony, Historic Blocs, and Capitalism: Antonio Gramsci in Library and Information Science," in *Critical Theory for Library and Information Science: Exploring the Social from Across the Disciplines*, eds. Gloria J. Leckie, Lisa M. Given, and John Buschman (Santa Barbara, CA: Libraries Unlimited, 2010), 149.

27. Karl Marx, "Theses on Feuerbach," in *The German* Ideology, by Karl Marx and Friedrich Engels (Amherst, NY: Prometheus Books, 1998),569.

instrument" that is "often of use just to show off learning."[28] He went on to note that such an approach is not dialectical, and that both criticism and self-criticism are revolutionary activities.[29] The philosopher, whether she is aware of it or not, *always* changes the world through the action of philosophizing, just as the "neutral" academic, whether she is aware of it or not, *always* has a political impact on the MCAL, even if that impact is solely to decelerate progressive change. According to Gramsci, the "consciousness of being a part of a particular hegemonic force (that is to say, political consciousness) is the first stage towards a further progressive self-consciousness in which theory and practice will finally be one."[30] Knowing this, the honest intellectual is the intellectual who theorizes while knowing that the act of theorizing has a material impact, and she owns it. Furthermore, she works to maximize this impact; that is, she works to change the world.

The reigning, dominant relations of both economic and cultural production in capitalism tend towards conservation. As I have argued thus far, capitalist society is riddled with contradictions that allow systemic exploitation to flourish, reproduce, and appear natural and inflexible. Furthermore, these skewed social relations are protected by an ideological façade that makes them appear natural, ideal, and sanctified by both religious and philosophical ideological norms. The very fact that unhealthy consciousness exists, whether it is the subservient consciousness of what Freire termed the "oppressed" (the dominated classes) or the dominating consciousness of the "oppressors" (the dominant class),[31] imputes that humans have the capacity to develop healthy consciousness, i.e., a critical consciousness that both understands the constructed nature of reality as well as the capacity to transform both oneself and reality. Accepting the material nature of mind and its related phenomena

---

28. Moacir Gadotti, *Pedagogy of Praxis: A Dialectical Philosophy of Education* (Albany, NY: State University of New York Press, 1996), 29.

29. Ibid., 30.

30. Gramsci, *Prison Notebooks*, 333.

31. Freire, *Pedagogy of the Oppressed*, 32-33.

as material allows one to see ideology as a material confluence of both physical matter and ideas, what Althusser said was a "material existence."[32] It also lets one see both how such material confluences can become fixed and how conscious material action, or praxis, can change material reality by affecting ideas and physical material. In short, although the MCAL as an organization strives towards relative stability through the dual action of reproducing society in order to reproduce itself, it contains the seeds of its own change as well as the people for shepherding the process. These people are counter-hegemonic academic librarians.

Because she has developed and works to continuously refine her consciousness of these social contradictions, the counter-hegemonic academic librarian is able to critically appraise both the academic library as a capitalist institution as well as her own role as an information worker within this institution. This role, however, extends beyond a personal cognitive awareness of social imbalance and injustices. Simple non-dialectical awareness of injustice certainly results in concerned, liberal progressive librarians, but does not necessarily result in action. The counter-hegemonic academic librarian *actively works to alter these underlying social relations by means of her professional labors* and, therefore, she works to effect material changes in the structure of the academic library as an institution. She does this through the understanding and systematic application of theory, as well as by being willing to transform this theory when it is called for.

Dialectical materialism is a robust theoretical apparatus that facilitates engaging in a dynamic progressive reflection that Freire termed *conscientização*, a progressive, theoretically conscious practice based on constant reflection, dialogue, and action. *Conscientização* is the antithesis of activism, the latter being what Freire called "naïve thinking," which is carried out in the MCAL by those who I referred to above as the "concerned liberal progressive librarians":

---

32. Louis Althusser, "Ideology and Ideological State Apparatuses: Notes towards an Investigation," in *Lenin and Philosophy and Other Essays*, trans. Ben Brewster (New York: Monthly Review Press, 2001), 112.

> Finally, true dialogue cannot exist unless the dialoguers engage in critical thinking—thinking which discerns an indivisible solidarity between the world and men admits of no dichotomy between them—thinking which perceives reality as process, as transformation, rather than as a static entity—thinking which does not separate itself from action, but constantly immerses itself in temporality without fear of the risks involved. Critical thinking contrasts with naïve thinking, which sees "historical time as a weight, a stratification of the acquisitions and experiences of the past," from which the present shall emerge normalized and "well-behaved."[33]

Freire's articulation of dialectics and educational praxis has much to offer those who desire to engage in transformative librarianship; the counter-hegemonic librarian is she who actively cultivates *conscientização*. Suffice it to say here that if we take Freire's distinction between *conscientização* and naïve thinking as two primary orientations towards navigating modern reality, then large swaths of humanity, perhaps the majority, fall into the latter category of naïve thinkers. This conclusion is not meant as an insult aimed at the majority, but a commentary on how people of all sorts are conditioned by history, culture, and perceived expediency. Naïve thinking is about (hopefully) pragmatic action in a society that does not value and reward things that contradict the conventional wisdom of capitalism; it works well as a way to maneuver in a fast-paced modern world where critical reflection and critically informed action has the potential to create roadblocks for the subject. Naïve thinking is not, however, a robust praxis; it artificially separates theory from action, which in turn weakens both theory and action. In contrast, *conscientização* accounts for theory as action.

Tipping the Scale

The dialectical materialist monist viewpoint that I have advocated for in this book requires that the intellectually honest library practitioner

---

33. Paulo Freire, *Pedagogy of the Oppressed*, 80-81. Material in quotations is, according to Freire in fn. 5, page 81, "from the letter of a friend."

considers the library as part of a complex network of relations that inextricably binds it with the greater sociopolitical environment. The counter-hegemonic librarian understands that many social relations, particularly those relations that support the dominant classes, are moribund and that such relations cannot exist indefinitely without eventual demands for change, crises, and the reactionary pushback that comes with these things. Such social relations are, at the very least, restrictive and/or counterproductive. For instance, even though a silent consensus may exist among a particular library faculty concerning the need to work for the equitable treatment of an underrepresented or underprivileged group—e.g., the LGBT community—institutionalized bias at the university or state level, a bias that in fact may be traced to the total ideology of capitalism, can discourage and hinder effective organization on the part of the librarians. In worst case scenarios, inequitable social relations may result in reactionary actions that lead to the persistence of oppression and reinforce already existing exploitative structures within the sociocultural milieu. The censorship of library materials that give views running counter to the values expressed by the dominant ideological forms, as well as the disproportionate inclusion of literature condemning the ideas, values, or even the existence of the subcultural or countercultural other, may have deleterious effects on students' understanding of diversity as well as their tolerance for difference. Members of these subcultural or countercultural groups may feel misrepresented, socially stifled, and even actively oppressed by the existence of a campus knowledgebase that excludes them and may even actively work against both their education and their general welfare. This is just one politically prominent current example.

    Accepting that capitalist social formations are exploitative, and that the MCAL supports this exploitation in its role as a conservative artificer of the status quo, the question then becomes: what should be done about the MCAL? The answer lies in coming to grips with the fact that academic libraries support the existence of multiple competing ideological frameworks apart from the dominant one, then accepting that certain ideological frameworks promote more equitable social associations, and then committing to actively supporting an ideological shift internally within the MCAL to one of these more equitable ideological frameworks. Doing these things will likewise support an ideological shift in the larger sociocultural environment. All of this requires understanding and implementing dialectical motion. The goal is to move the institution away from the dominant, conservative paradigm towards its antithesis. That is, to tip the MCAL into meaningful counter-hegemony.

Chapter 6

THE TRANSITION OF QUANTITY INTO QUALITY AS A TOOL FOR COUNTER-HEGEMONY

In this chapter I examine how a dialectical process, the principle of the transformation of quantity into quality, works in the MCAL. I do this in order to show how coming to understand dialectical change may empower critical analysts and provide them with tools to strategize actions.

This basic dialectical principle of development holds that all human social relations possess two contradictory opposites, expressed by quantity and quality. As with everything dialectical, quantity and quality are intimately related, and changes in one results in changes to the other, and vice versa. The addition or subtraction of quantitative units to a magnitude in relation to a particular material phenomenon, therefore, may result in a sudden change to that phenomenon's qualitative organization, causing a radical transformation in the whole. Engels sometimes referenced the relationship between temperature and water when giving an example of this dialectical principle. Water remains in an essentially stable form as heat is applied to it, at least until the temperature reaches 100°C. At water's boiling point, which is the result of a quantitative accretion of heat, the liquid undergoes a rapid change in quality, becoming water vapor.[1] Conversely, when heat is removed from liquid water, it

---

1. Friedrich Engels, *Dialectics of Nature*, ed. and trans. Clemens Dutt (New York: International Publishers, 1940), 29-30.

remains in the same form until another quantitative threshold has been reached—0°C—at which point the water becomes ice.

In relation to human social reality, as well as being closely related to academia and scientific communication, Kuhn's theory of change in science is a classic example of the transition of quantity into quality. Kuhn argued that scientific theory and practice operate within structurally defined models in which practitioners of a mature science actively engage in normal puzzle-solving behavior, i.e., "normal science." However, at the same time that this routine and dominant scientific theory and practice is occurring, a small but growing number of bold scientists act as a vanguard, engaging in a cutting-edge research, i.e., revolutionary science. Revolutionary science challenges the dominant scientific paradigm through exposing anomalies in its fundamental theories. The dual action of normal and revolutionary science continues, often to the detriment of the cutting-edge scientists who may be relegated to the fringes of their discipline because of resistance to change. At times, however, the challenges raised by this vanguard's work, as well as the increasing number of converts to the revolutionary scientists' ideas concerning the structural bases of a discipline, may result in a dramatic shift in which the perceived foundations of a discipline's theories are upended and replaced with new theoretical structures. Kuhn discussed various possible impetuses for this process, one being that the process *builds* to the paradigm shift, often over a period of many years. A threat to normal science grows as the anomaly gains exposure. This exposure causes the literature of revolutionary science to snowball. More and more renowned scientists begin to subscribe to the position espoused by the revolutionary science and to weigh in on the position,[2] and "by proliferating versions of the paradigm, crisis loosens the rules of normal puzzle-solving in ways that ultimately permit a new paradigm to emerge."[3] This momentum and accumulation of "competing articulations" leads

---

2. Thomas S. Kuhn, *The Structure of Scientific Revolutions*, 3rd ed. (Chicago, IL: University of Chicago Press, 1996), 82.

3. Ibid., 80.

to a fundamental shift in the types of questions asked, as well as how these questions are approached.[4] Kuhn offered many examples of this transition from quantity to quality within the framework of scientific revolutions, the most famous being the shift from the Aristotelian, Earth-centered model of the solar system, a model which had existed for millennia, to the Copernican, heliocentric model. He also pointed to "typical" examples of the paradigm shift following a "breakdown and proliferation of [revolutionary] theories,"[5] including the discovery of oxygen in the eighteenth century and the development of the theory of relativity in the late-nineteenth century. Kuhn's theory of scientific revolution should be heartening to the counter-hegemonic academic librarian in that it describes how heterodox professional intellectual work may lead to substantive change through dedicated incremental activity.

Another example of a quantitative to qualitative shift in the sphere of human cognitive transformation which is relatable to the experience of most people, is the sudden cognitive understanding achieved through continued academic study, i.e., when a subject goes quickly from cognitive dissonance to understanding, when it all comes together and clicks. For instance, when a student engages with a particular discipline, e.g., cultural studies, she may feel that she consumes information regarding cultural studies with little progress. At some point, after being exposed to pertinent disciplinary concepts through frequent and repetitive contact, the subject matter clicks and the student quickly reaches a lucid understanding of the subject that had previously been elusive. Concepts that may have long been muddy suddenly become clear, as do the relationships between various concepts. The subject area as a whole takes on a new meaning. A similar phenomenon has been hypothesized to occur when people learn second languages. Cummins found that, at a point in learning a new language, i.e., when an adequate level of proficiency has been realized in both the first *and* second languages, the student

---

4. Ibid., 91.
5. Ibid., 75.

crosses a minimum threshold of experience after which they rapidly achieve competence.[6]

The character of academic librarianship has undergone dramatic structural changes in the last few hundred years or so, and these changes may be traced in part to the transition of quantity into quality. Prior to the industrial revolution, librarianship had been a primarily male-dominated semi-profession. This changed, however, in the second half of the nineteenth century with the development of professional programs in librarianship, programs that produced a large number of female graduates, transforming librarianship into a "women's profession."[7] The feminization of librarianship, however, may be seen in terms of broader dialectic-historical processes. The industrial revolution shifted the roles of men and women in the work force, with many women extending beyond their traditional roles of maintaining the family household to occupying labor positions in the industrial workforce. In *Wage-Labour and Capital*, Marx wrote that, as the mass of women and children enter the work force, they are exploited to assume positions formerly held by adult males.[8] The recent history of academic libraries offers examples of the transition of quantity into quality. Many instances of this process are directly related to LIS's intimate relationship with information technology and the rapid development of computing technology in the last fifty years. One example that academic librarians are presently dealing with is the Open Access (OA) movement. OA is a recent trend in academic publishing that is rapidly restructuring the terrain of scholarly communication and, as a result, is of great concern to academic librarians. In the OA model, scholarly publications are made available online free of charge to the information consumer, although the author may

---

6. Jim Cummins, *Language, Power and Pedagogy: Bilingual Children in the* Crossfire (Clevedon, UK: Multilingual Matters, 2000), 37.

7. Barbara Elizabeth Brand, "Sex-Typing in Education for Librarianship: 1870-1920," in *The Status of Women in Librarianship: Historical, Sociological, and Economic Issues*, ed. Kathleen M. Heim (New York: Neal-Schuman, 1983), 29.

8. Karl Marx, *Wage-Labour and Capital* (New York: International Publishers, 1933), 46-47.

be charged a fee. OA began slowly in the 1990s with only a few freely available publications and much trepidation on the part of researchers to publish in these outlets. However, the slow expansion in the number of pure OA (i.e., those outlets that provide free access to all articles) and hybrid OA (i.e., those outlets that provide free access to certain articles but require a subscription to view others) publishers has, particularly over the last decade or so, seen rapid growth. The number of published Gold OA articles, those articles made freely available to readers but with a cost to authors, have seen remarkable growth. For example, in a study of OA journals from 1993-2009, Laakso et al. found that the "journal count for the year 2000 is estimated to have been 740, and 4769 for 2009,"[9] an increase of 544% over ten years. Dramatic increases in the complexity, distribution, and application of information technology have picked up momentum to make for a very different publishing landscape than just a few years prior. Combine this increase in technological innovation with the quantitative spread of an ideology of Open Access, such as with major institutional pushes like Harvard University's adoption of an OA publishing requirement for all of its researchers, and a tipping point may soon be reached in which the nature of scholarly publishing is transformed into a completely new, qualitatively different model. This qualitative shift, very importantly, has been *anticipated*, allowing for both professional planning and efforts to guide the new publishing model's material realization. Lewis, for example, wrote that, by the year 2020, OA will be "the dominant model for scholarly journals and will represent a growing portion of scholarship of all kinds."[10] The ability to anticipate a future paradigm shift, combined with an effective theoretico-practical approach—praxis—demonstrates the value of a critical approach to library and information science as a transformational tool. While changes

---

9. Mikael Laakso and others, "The Development of Open Access Journal Publishing from 1993 to 2009," *PLoS ONE* 6, no. 6 (2011), http://journals.plos.org/plosone/article?id=10.1371/journal.pone.0020961.

10. David W. Lewis, "From Stacks to the Web: The Transformation of Academic Library Collecting," *College & Research Libraries* 74, no. 2 (March 2013), 173.

in libraries and librarianship that may be attributed to this transition of quantity into quality have often blindsided library practitioners, dialectical materialism is a means for both prediction and strategic action.

How can counter-hegemonic academic librarians use their knowledge of this dialectical movement? Careful analysis of present circumstances and historical context, even when not applying a developed critical/cultural method or ideology like Marxist, feminist, or queer theory, allows for the diagnosis of library-related transformations and the careful design of strategies in lieu of a projected future. Another example of the transition from quantity to quality, one that has been recognized and represents an example of a conscious approach to a perceived problematic future, is the recognition of the digital dark age and attempts to remedy the impending situation. The digital dark age refers to one such situation in which a future transition of quantity to quality has been recognized, and this realization has inspired much discussion and effort to preempt such an event from occurring. The digital dark age refers to the looming possibility that, as media storage formats shift the bulk of stored information to increasingly ephemeral types of media (e.g., the steamrolling transition from print to digital format for serials and monographs), a point will be reached when the increasing fragility and turnover of new formats leads to a sudden massive loss of recorded information. That is, that at some point changes in information technology will so greatly outstrip our ability for administrative and preservationist adaptation that we will suffer the deterioration of both learning and culture. Librarians seem to be intuitively aware of this basic dialectical principle and have begun initiating change to countermand the digital dark age as a result of this intuition.

The concept that at some point quantitative increase or decrease results in an intrinsic change in quality should be considered optimistically by those practitioners who hope to harness materialist dialectics for progressive ends and real material change. In terms of praxis, accepting the viability of this dialectical principle allows for a practical-theoretical confidence. It suggests that the constant and rigorous application of theoretically based social interventions will ultimately lead to a paradigm shift in the institution in question. The progressive academic librarian, as a result of this confidence, can develop, apply, and actively promote and spread mediating techniques, assuming the strategy that at some point addition or subtraction will result in needed change.

Chapter 7

CONCLUSIONS (AND BEGINNINGS)

From experience, the academic librarian is aware of the vast number of physical objects that make up the MCAL. The library is much more than a collection of books but also includes buildings, academic journals, popular magazines, maps, compact discs, vinyl records, coffee mugs, computer hardware, and computer software. As a result of this great assortment of physical objects, it can be hard to determine the actual physical limits of the academic library. Do we conceive of the library as including the World Wide Web? Do we include the gallons of coffee consumed inside the library's walls? In this book, I have contended that the answer to all of the above questions is yes. The library is much more than the physical. We should think expansively about the academic library as a flexible body composed of many physical objects, but in order to grasp the institution in its entirety, we cannot focus solely on its corporeal elements. If we limit our theoretical considerations of the academic library to a purely physical understanding of what constitutes its material presence, we risk becoming stuck in a scientistic and mechanistic rut that will result in a flawed and narrow understanding of the institution. Such routes to understanding handicap our capacity for constructive criticism of the academic library as a social reality with complex spatial and temporal consequences. Do the limits of the academic library as an institution actually extend to include everything that exists? Do they conform to my contention that libraries are "the material interaction of both mental concepts and physical objects as they mesh together in human culture and history as material presence"? If so, what does this mean? The gallons of coffee drunk in the academic library, the empty pizza boxes left in the stacks, even the thousands of pages of marginalia scrawled in the books in the stacks, all contribute to the academic library's composition. To best understand this complexity, we must extend our imagination beyond parochial views of the library as either a grand idea or as a defined collection of "library-esque" physical objects. The marginalia in a library's collection of books, for instance, are significant not only because of their impact on the library as a materially physical presence (evidenced by the damage that they inflict on the books). These embellishments to books are also important as ideas, even if only to a tiny degree, in the total constitution of the library. Both library books and their marginalia are memorials to the past use of the library collection for knowledge creation and transformation, as well as potential elements of future transformative dialogue.[1] They can even boost the auction price of rare books.

Dialectics accounts for the vigorous and perpetual change occurring in the real world. In this way, it not only serves as a means for understanding the MCAL as a living institution woven into a greater, infinitely dynamic existence, it also provides a cognitive standpoint and mode of practice from which practicing librarians may actively confront and change this dynamic existence. Approaching the world dialectically, however, seems alien to many people; it is not straightforward in terms of cause and effect, and it appears to provide little comfort to those people seeking stability in terms of their known realities, at least initially. But once a dialectical understanding of reality has been sufficiently grasped and internalized by the critical analyst, it becomes difficult—it even begins to seem absurd—to revert to traditional logics and ontologies that do not account for change and that, upon reflection, always seem to end up validating the status quo. Such reflection quickly leads to the insight that status quos are ultimately ephemeral conditions that, despite all of the best efforts of the dominant interests which they

---

1. H. J. Jackson, *Marginalia: Readers Writing in Books* (New Haven, CT: Yale University Press, 2001), 234.

benefit, inevitably run their course. At that point they are remembered with either a sort of impotent nostalgia or a modernist disdain.

Therefore, when approaching the MCAL dialectically, the institution becomes more than a fixed entity or idea. Instead, the MCAL is experienced as a phenomenon that is forever in process. More precisely, the library is experienced as a set of relations. That is, the MCAL and the phenomena that surround it, interact with it, fall inside of its orbit, and pull it into their own orbits, are experienced as a set of fluid social relations constantly in the act of becoming. As a set of social relations, the MCAL is in a state of constant motion and perpetual transformation that explodes our traditionally held ideas concerning its composition and boundaries. When the MCAL is conceived as concrete relations, it is no longer constrained by the limitations imposed on it by positivist restrictions that choose to ignore mental phenomena or that impose an artificial separation between the mental and the physical world, two modes of thought that seem to be so entrenched in modern humanity's approach to knowledge. Instead, the MCAL may be conceptualized as a fluctuating institution or set of institutions that are organic to neoliberal capitalist society and woven directly into this society. If the critical analyst takes the viewpoint that her reality is, at the same time, a singular entirety and a diffuse system of interpenetrating individualities, the MCAL must be considered as part of this greater sociocultural entirety.

In this book, I have attempted to show the profoundly contradictory nature of the library, that while academic librarians navigate a social environment that produces an extensive amount of rhetoric centering on concepts like Democracy, Equality, and Self-determination, the MCAL also maintains an organizational structure that is vertical, hierarchical, and patriarchal. The inherent contradictions found in the present capitalist society writ large, and focused and observable in the MCAL, insure the exploitation of classes within society. For example, the concept of the growing digital divide, i.e., that the proliferation of new information technology excludes the economically disadvantaged from knowledge acquisition, and thus the ability to improve their economic condition, is an intrinsic problem within the MCAL, compounded by its other exclusionary aspects (tuition; lack of services to community users, etc.).

When we lose historical perspective, the MCAL becomes not only disassociated from humanity, but alienated from it. Jorge Luis Borges, himself a former librarian, set forth his devastating personal vision of paradise lost in his "Poem about Gifts." Written as he was losing his sight, the poem depicts Borges's final alienation from his library:

> As I walk through the slow galleries
> I grow to feel with a kind of holy dread
> That I am the other, I am the dead,
> And the steps I make are also his.[2]

This despairing verse may be seen as a metaphor for many library users' separation from the academic library by idealisms, ideologies, and alienation. These obstructions are long-held and historically ingrained. They are, nonetheless, capable of being countered and removed.

Kick Out the Jams

As a means of critical analysis, dialectical materialism is a rational path for both analyzing the structures that underlie the current expression of prevailing relations of power and working towards equality. This final chapter is not meant to signal a conclusion to anything. Indeed, to fully embrace dialectics means to reject finalities. This book is meant to facilitate ongoing inquiry and to move forward a discussion of the academic library as a social institution, academic librarianship as a profession, and the role of academic librarians as social actors and change agents who possess the ability to accomplish things of great social consequence. This book is a point of entry into a discussion about the material realities of where we work and what we do.

---

2. Jorge Luis Borges, "Poem of the Gifts," in *Dream Tigers*, trans. Mildred Boyer and Harold Morland (Austin, TX: University of Texas Press, 1965), 55.

CONCLUSIONS (AND BEGINNINGS)   153

Why should one adopt a progressive approach to knowledge acquisition and action? Pannekoek pointed out that there are certain characteristics that distinguish human beings from animals, including their ability to think abstractly, their conscious use of tools, and their ability to speak.[3] These three characteristics work together in a dialectical fashion to illuminate another characteristic that distinguishes human beings from animals: the ability and tendency towards progress that extends beyond biological evolution and one that extends through human ingenuity and society: "only man has a continuous history: His history is one of a constant advance and unfolding, at an increasingly rapid rate."[4] Similarly, Lenin wrote that "the world does not satisfy man and man decides to change it by his activity."[5] This last goal, the practical transformation of reality, should be the goal of any professional activity, and this should be the case whether or not the professional adheres to any sort of critical philosophy. The goal of medical practitioners is to increase the physical and mental well-being of humankind. The goal of clergy people is to improve humanity's spiritual welfare and spur their spiritual development. For lawyers, it is to maximize the law's potential towards social justice. Academic librarians also possess a normative goal. I propose that academic librarians' goal, at its most general, is to maintain humanity's knowledge welfare by working to eliminate their alienation from information and knowledge, an alienation that the MCAL accomplishes quite effectively and opaquely. In their capacity as gatekeepers of information, academic librarians possess a much broader scope of influence than physicians, clergy, and many educators.

Even though humans seem predisposed towards progress, they also ceaselessly undermine this progress through violence and oppression. Materialist dialectics is a path through reality that accounts for this contradiction and sets out to realize humankind's potential for positive

---

3. Anton Pannekoek, *Anthropogenesis: A Study of the Origin of Man* (Amsterdam: North-Holland Publishing Company, 1953), 105.

4. Ibid., 88.

5. V. I. Lenin, *Philosophical Notebooks, Collected Works,* vol. 38, ed. Stewart Smith, trans. Clemence Dutt, (Moscow: Progress Publishers, 1976), 213.

transformation by means of the refinement available through praxis. On a gut level, today's academic librarians seem to intuitively grasp that the contradiction of motion and stasis is a pervasive and permanent feature of their work lives and that their job both focuses the contradiction and cycles between its extremities.

Realistically, what can be done? Sweeping structural change in modern capitalist society has proven to be an immensely difficult task. The structure of society is bolstered by the deeply engrained capitalist *Weltanschauung* that stretches across class boundaries. Nonetheless, if one adopts the viewpoint that everything that exists, both material and cognitive, is in constant connection, then it becomes necessary to question why the MCAL supports the status quo. In addition, such introspection also leads to an understanding of the ultimate permeability of the MCAL's role in reproducing this *Weltanschauung* and supporting the status quo, and to prompt the professional librarian to explore alternatives to this function. A broad culture of critique of the MCAL and academic librarianship would potentially lead to a broad culture of change within the library. This change, furthermore, would be largely inimical to the existing social conditions that implement the MCAL as a maintenance tool.

In order to transform society in a progressive fashion, one must possess and maintain a basic faith in the possibility of sweeping, progressive change (with the maintenance aspect of faith being a substantially more difficult task than simply the possession of faith). Upon committing to the transformation of the MCAL and committing to serve as an impetus for this change, how do academic librarians accomplish meaningful transformation within and through the MCAL? The idea that strategic changes within the library as an institution may both disrupt and reorganize the equilibrium of the societal entirety, and do so as a benefit to human equality and freedom, is of enormous importance to the practicing academic librarian, keeping in mind that she is a professional who is devoted to public service and is obligated to achieve these two concepts, even if keeping good faith comes at the expense of the basic tenets of the prevailing dominant ideology.

Appendix

Resources for the Counter-Hegemonic Academic Librarian

This appendix collects resources for counter-hegemonic academic librarians. It is divided into five primary sections, each consisting of an alphabetized list of briefly annotated citations. In constructing and ordering these lists I have sought to remain as consistent as possible with the general structure of this book. The first section collects literature that focuses on both general examinations of materialist dialectics as well as the relevant literature that relates materialist dialectics directly to LIS related topics. The second section does the same for general and LIS related materials concerning ideology. Section 3 collects literature related to professional praxis and transformative education and pedagogy. Section 4 is a list of online resources for progressive information workers. These bibliographic lists are in no way meant to be comprehensive. They are meant to be taken as recommended points of entry to the critical analysis of LIS study.

1. Resources Pertaining to Dialectical Materialism, the MCAL, and Academic Librarianship

The literature relating to dialectical materialism that is meaningful to the study of the MCAL mirrors the far-reaching and profoundly discursive nature of the MCAL as an institution. That is, valuable literature is interwoven within and between diverse subject areas. In order to gain a perspicuous understanding of the dialectical nature of the MCAL, and in order to accumulate the knowledge necessary to best engage in transformative praxis, readers must read widely and far afield. The following list of citations related to dialectical materialism is composed of the following parts: (a) starting places for expanding theoretical consciousness and (b) texts that relate dialectical thinking to LIS.

(a) Expanding Theoretical Consciousness

- Bekerman, Gerard. *Marx and Engels: A Conceptual Concordance.* Translated by Terrell Carver. Totowa, NJ: Barnes & Noble Books, 1983. This is an essential reference tool for anyone researching Marx and Engels, providing entries for all of the major philosophical concepts found in these philosophers' writings with page pointers to the Standard English translations of their major works, as well as cross-references to related concepts.

- Carver, Terrell. *A Marx Dictionary.* Totowa, NJ: Barnes & Noble Books, 1987. This short subject dictionary provides clear and concise explanations of important technical concepts as used by Marx, including such terms as "capitalism," "exploitation," and "base and superstructure." Each entry provides direct references to Marx's original writing as well as reading lists that point to important secondary sources.

- Dietzgen, Joseph. *The Nature of Human Brainwork: An Introduction to Dialectics.* Oakland, PA: PM Press 2010. This book is the major exposition of Dietzgen's thought. It affirms many of the primary features of Marx and Engel's thought while being free of much of the dogma that was later built up around Marxism.

- Engels, Friederich. *Socialism: Utopian and Scientific.* New York: International Publishers, 2004. Unlike Marx, Engels wrote profusely on materialist dialectic *qua* method. This book is an abbreviated version of his polemical *Anti-Dühring*. It contains chapters on utopian socialism, the materialist conception of history, and scientific socialism. It is written for a popular audience and is highly suggested as a starting point.

- Harvey, David. *Seventeen Contradictions and the End of Capitalism*. Oxford, UK: Oxford University Press, 2014. This recent classic, written from the perspective of a Marxist geographer, incorporates dialectical reasoning into an analysis of the late-capitalist economy.

- Krapivin, Vassilii. *What is Dialectical Materialism?* Moscow: Progress Publishers, 1985. The Soviet "ABCs" are popular treatments of dialectical and historical materialism, that, while they do not venture far from late mainline Soviet dogma and one should view them with a critical eye, are easy to read and concise. This work is particularly valuable for its glossary of philosophical terms.

- Lenin, V. I. *Materialism and Empirio-Criticism: Critical Comments on a Reactionary Philosophy*. New York: International Publishers, 1972. Despite being a tedious polemic against Ernst Mach's subjective idealism, this work provides valuable explanations of dialectical materialism, comparing it to idealism, rationalism, and empiricism.

- Marx, Karl. *Capital: A Critique of the Political Economy*, Volume I. Translated by Ben Fowkes. London: Penguin Books, 1976. This book remains the best example of Marx applying his dialectical method to the study of capitalism. *Capital* is both a compelling critical examination and a sharp indictment of the capitalist society in which Marx lived.

- Ollman, Bertell. *Dance of the Dialectic: Steps in Marx's Method.* Urbana, IL: University of Illinois Press, 2003. Ollman rigorously describes and renders a heuristic explanation of Marx's method. This book provides examples of dialectic's application to real-world situations.

- Resnick, Stephen A. and Richard D. Wolff, eds. *New Departures in Marxian Theory.* London: Routledge, 2006. The essays in this volume offer a post-Althussarian reading of materialist dialectic that consider concepts like overdetermination.

(b) Resources that Relate Critical Thinking to LIS

- Budd, John M. *Self-Examination: The Present and Future of Librarianship.* Westport, CT: Libraries Unlimited, 2008. This work is a critical analysis of libraries past and present. Of particular interest is Budd's consideration of the role of the library in the neoliberal present.

- Crowley, Bill. *Spanning the Theory-Practice Divide in Library & Information Science.* Lanham, MD: Scarecrow Press, 2005. Crowley examines the modern librarian as both academic and practitioner within the context of neo-liberal society.

- Dick, Archie L. "Epistemological Positions and Library and Information Science." *Library Quarterly* 69, no. 3 (1999): 305-323. This article considers epistemological positions taken in LIS. Dick proposes holistic perspectivism as a framework for accommodating these multiple epistemologies in LIS.

- Fuchs, Christian. *Foundations of Critical Media and Information Studies.* London: Routledge, 2011. Fuchs uses a Marxist critique of 21st century information technologies. Topics of interest to academic librarians include web 2.0, social networking sites, and intellectual property rights.

- Lua, Gregory and Shana Higgins, eds. *Information Literacy and Social Justice: Radical Professional Praxis.* Sacramento, CA: Library Juice Press, 2013. Inspired by the work of Freire and Giroux, this book collects articles concerning information literacy under neoliberalism, critical pedagogy, and community engagement.

- Leckie, Gloria J., and John E. Buschman, eds. *Information Technology in Librarianship: New Critical Approaches.* Westport, CT: Libraries Unlimited, 2009. The essays in this edited collection explore the impact of information technology on the library community from many different critical perspectives including Marxism, feminism, and critical legal studies.

- Leckie, Gloria J., Lisa M. Given, and John E. Buschman, eds. *Critical Theory for Library and Information Science: Exploring the Social from Across the Disciplines.* Santa Barbara, CA: Libraries Unlimited, 2003. This edited collection presents valuable readings that relate particular critical and cultural theorists to LIS. The discipline is examined through the theoretical lenses of such luminaries as Marx, Lefebvre, Latour, and Heidegger.

- Maxwell, Nancy Kalikow. *Sacred Stacks: The Higher Purpose of Libraries and Librarianship.* Chicago, IL: American Library Association, 2006. Maxwell analyzes libraries and librarianship through the lens of religion. Covering a wide range of topics tying the library to the holy, this fascinating little book includes discussions about the library's role in organizing society and the library as sacred space.

- Wisner, William H. *Whither the Postmodern Library? Libraries, Technology, and Education in the Information Age.* Jefferson, NC: McFarland & Company, 1999. This book provides a commentary on the impact of new information technology on the character of the late-twentieth century library, written by a traditionalist librarian.

2. Resources for Developing a Consciousness of Ideology and Its Institutional Apparatuses

The MCAL is an ISA that serves to maintain the dominant ideology through reproducing the prevailing sociocultural norms and hegemonic structures. The following literature provides analyses of ideology and ideological structures both generally and as related to LIS and information work.

- Althusser, Louis. *For Marx.* Translated by Ben Brewster. London: Penguin Press, 1965. Althusser's famous essay critiquing and revising the base/superstructure, "Overdetermination and Contradiction," can be found here.

- ———. *On the Reproduction of Capitalism: Ideology and Ideological State Apparatuses.* London: Verso, 2014. This is an excellent encapsulation of Althusser's thought on ISAs and includes essays on the ideology's relationship to philosophy, production and reproduction, law, and the state. This book includes his famous essay "Ideology and Ideological State Apparatuses."

- Dilevko, Juris, and Lisa Gottlieb. "The Politics of Standard Selection Guides: The Case of the *Public Library Catalog.*" *Library Quarterly* 73, no. 3 (2003): 289-337. This examination of a standard collection development resource for public libraries reveals underlying ideological frames. Dilevko and Gottlieb warn that such tools may lead to the "McDonaldization" of the library.

- Doherty, John. "The Academic Librarian and the Hegemony of the Canon." *Journal of Academic Librarianship* 24, no. 5 (1998): 403-406. This article looks at the development of standard canons and their relationship with collection development and the hegemonic determination of disciplines. Doherty argues that libraries should use their collection development responsibilities to actively mold canons of literature to be more inclusive and counter-hegemonic.

- Feather, John P. *The Information Society: A Study of Continuity and Change*, 6th edition. London: Facet, 2013. Contains analyses of the development of information in society, mass media and new technology, information economics, politics, information and the state, and information workers in modern society.

- Freeden, Michael. *Ideology: A Very Short Introduction*. Oxford: Oxford University Press. 2003. This very readable book outlines the major theories of ideology, including those of Marx, Gramsci, Mannheim, and Althusser, giving particular attention to the relationship between ideology and politics.

- Giroux, Henry A. *Border Crossings: Cultural Workers and the Politics of Education*. 2nd ed. New York: Routledge, 2005. Giroux is a leading exponent of critical pedagogy in the United States who has authored over 60 books. This book examines the relationships between educators and politics. This edition has been updated to include considerations of pedagogy in the post-9/11 world.

- Gramsci, Antonio. *Selections from the Prison Notebooks.* Edited and translated by Quinton Hoare and Geoffrey Nowell Smith. New York: International Publishers, 1971. Writing from prison, Gramsci developed his ideas concerning hegemony and the role of the intellectual in society.

- Kranich, Nancy, ed. *Libraries & Democracy: The Cornerstones of Liberty.* Chicago: American Library Association, 2001. Although most of the book is aimed at mainstream progressive librarians, many of the ideas put forward are of use to more radical approaches to librarianship.

- Mannheim, Karl. *Ideology & Utopia: An Introduction to the Sociology of Knowledge.* San Diego, CA: Harcourt. 1936. This work was a major step in the theory of ideology that addressed the Marxist false consciousness/science dichotomy, while clearly being influenced by it. Mannheim offers a totalizing view of ideology founded on his concept of "relational knowledge."

- Marx, Karl and Friedrich Engels. *The German Ideology.* Amherst, NY: Prometheus Books, 1998. This book, first published in full in 1932, explicates Marx and Engels's view of ideology as false consciousness.

- Stevenson, Siobhan. "Digital Divide: A Discursive Move Away from the Real Inequities." *Information Society* 25 (2009): 1-22. Stevenson unpacks the meaning of the "Digital Divide" in neoliberal societies, arguing that neoliberal ideology has shifted the discourse and perceptions surrounding the issue away from its connections with class struggle.

3. Resources for Approaching the MCAL as a Terrain of Struggle

Although LIS research is still largely enthralled with quantitative approaches and a scientific method that artificially separates theory from practice, there is much good work that investigates librarianship as a progressive praxis for transformative education in ways that may be easily applied to library environments. This work extends into many areas of practice including library instruction, collection development, user advocacy, adult education, and community development.

- Accardi, Maria T., Emily Drabinski, and Alana Kumbier, eds. *Critical Library Instruction: Theories and Methods.* Duluth, MN: Library Juice Press, 2010. This edited collection provides a variety of perspectives rooted in critical theory that will help inform conscious approaches to library instruction. The essays provide broad theoretical analyses and offer practical strategies for engaging in critical pedagogy.

- American Library Association. *Intellectual Freedom Manual.* 8th ed. Chicago: American Library Association, 2010. This convenient volume collects the American Library Association's major policy statements and resolutions regarding intellectual freedom and related issues, as well as historical material, interpretations, and essays concerning these items.

- Aronowitz, Stanley, and Henry A. Giroux. *Education Still under Seige.* 2nd ed. Westport, CT: Bergin & Garvey, 1993. Aronowitz and Giroux lay out their vision concerning transformational intellectuals and radical pedagogy. This is an important update and application of the work of theorists like Gramsci and Freire to modern education.

- Bosaller, Jenny, Denice Adkins, and Kim M. Thompson. "Critical Theory, Libraries and Culture." *Progressive Librarian* 34-35 (2010): 25-38. Adkins et al. analyze the role of the modern librarian—both public and academic—using the theoretical work of modern educational and sociological theorists, including Giroux, Marcuse, and Foucault, to argue that libraries in capitalist societies are a terrain of struggle between dominant and oppressed classes.

- Cyzyk, Mark. "Canon Formation, Library Collections, and the Dilemma of Collection Development." *College & Research Libraries* 54, no. 1 (1993): 58-65. Cyzyk discusses the social and ideological roles of both library collections and the librarians charged with these collections' development and maintenance.

- Edwards, Julie Biando. "Neutrality in Context: Principles and Rights." *Information for Social Change* 31 (2011): 17-27. Edwards examines the focus of the American Library Association's *Code of Ethics* on individual rights and argues that concepts of library neutrality tend to work in this context.

- Freire, Paulo. *Pedagogy of the Oppressed*. Translated by Myra Bergman Ramos. New York: Continuum, 1967. This is a classic work of modern critical theory and its practical transformative application to pedagogy. It discusses the concept of *conscientização* and gives insight into Freire's dialectics.

- Holt, Leslie Edmonds and Glen E. Holt. *Public Library Services for the Poor: Doing All We Can*. Chicago: American Library Association, 2010. Considering that many urban academic libraries serve large populations of the poor and the homeless, much of the information found here is easily transferrable to an academic setting.

APPENDIX: RESOURCES 167

- LaRue, James. *The New Inquisition: Understanding and Managing Intellectual Freedom Challenges.* Westport, CT: Libraries Unlimited, 2007. This is a practical guide for facing intellectual freedom issues in the public library, and has much parallel value to academic librarians. LaRue provides real-life examples of situations that librarians face, as well as sample documents and action strategies useful for weathering freedom challenges.

- Lewis, Alison, ed. *Questioning Library Neutrality: Essays from Progressive Librarian.* Duluth, MN: Library Juice, 2008. Librarian neutrality, which was once seemingly taken for granted, came to the forefront in the last half of the twentieth century and remains a heavily debated topic. This book collects essays previously published in the journal *Progressive Librarian* that consider modern librarians' relationship to neutrality and politics, and provides arguments for activism, praxis, and resistance to the dominant culture.

- Morrone, Melissa, and Lisa Friedman. "Radical Reference: Socially Responsible Librarianship Collaborating with Community." *The Reference Librarian* 50, no. 4 (2009): 371-396. This is an overview of the development, aims, and operations of the Radical Reference collective; it provides examples of successful initiatives and outreach efforts.

- McCook, Kathleen de la Peña. *A Place at the Table: Participating in Community Building.* Chicago: American Library Association, 2000. This book explores the role of American libraries within the broader communities that they serve and looks at ways for the library to take part in community-building initiatives.

- Robbins, Louise. *Censorship and the American Library: The American Library Association's Response to Threats to Intellectual Freedom, 1939-1969*. Westport, CT: Greenwood Press, 1996. This history chronicles American librarianship's relationship, through the work of professional associations like the ALA, as well as through the efforts of individual librarians, with intellectual freedom issues for a large portion of the mid-twentieth century.

- Samek, Toni. *Intellectual Freedom and Social Responsibility in American Librarianship, 1967-1974*. With a forward by Sanford Berman. Jefferson, NC: McFarland, 2001. Samek probes a transitional point in the history of librarianship in the United States, the period from 1967 to 1974, in which many American librarians questioned the profession's official position of neutrality. This book reinforces the notion that the modern library remains a field of struggle and that counterhegemonic opposition has flared up in the past and, at points, has achieved notable levels of organization.

- ———. "Ethical Reflections on 21st Century Information Work: An Address to Teachers and Librarians." *Progressive Librarian* 25 (Summer 2005): 43-62.

- Schwenk, Kim. "Another World Possible: Radical Archiving in the 21st Century." *Progressive Librarian* 36-37 (Fall 2011): 51-58. Schwenk examines radical archives in America, giving historical context and providing examples of archives operating from radical perspectives.

- Stienstra, Deborah. "The Critical Space Between: Access, Inclusion and Standards in Information Technologies." *Information Communication & Society* 9, no. 3 (2006): 335-354. This is an analysis of Canadian legislation meant to ensure disabled persons' access to information technologies. It critiques the influence of business interests on the development of compliancy standards, giving insight into the interconnectedness of governmental institutions, corporate interests, and, of interest to academic librarians, information technology.

- Venturella, Karen, ed. *Poor People and Library Services.* Jefferson, NC: McFarland, 1998. Poor people are too often discounted in both public and (some may contend more often) in academic libraries. This collection of essays addresses the obstacles that the poor face in gaining access to information and taking full advantage of library services. Sections include: "Theory and Background," "Poverty Programs for Children," "Access to Technology for Low-income Groups," "Neighborhood Coalition and International Organization," "Suggestions for Action," "Programs in Shelters and Public Housing," and "Rural Poverty Programs."

4. Online Resources for the Counter-hegemonic Academic Librarian

- Information for Social Change, URL: http://libr.org/isc/. Information for Social Change is a UK-based activist organization of information workers. The website acts as an online information clearing house for members as well as a platform for distributing its online journal, *Information for Social Change.*

- Marxists Internet Archive, URL: http://www.marxists.org. This is a massive collection of full-text Marxist (e.g., Marx, Engels, Lenin) literature and related works (e.g., Bakunin). Searchable by either author or subject.

- *Microaggressions in Librarianship*, http://lismicroaggressions.tumblr.com/. An online space for library workers belonging to marginalized groups to recount their personal experiences of work-related microaggressions. This site gives valuable insight into the subtle persistence of ideology in libraries.

- Radical Librarians Collective, URL: http://radicallibcamp.wikispaces.com/. A UK-based group that aims to connect radical librarians and to work against the corporatization of the modern library.

- Progressive Librarians Guild, URL: http://www.progressivelibrariansguild.org/. The PLG is a long-running organization that focuses on advancing social justice and progressive change in information institution of all sorts. This site provides news, information concerning PLG chapters, and access to the PLG-sponsored journal, *Progressive Librarian*.

- Radical Reference, URL: http://radicalreference.info/. This group started in 2004 and spawned local collectives nationally and internationally. Although the Radical Reference website no longer provides answers to reference questions, it does provide links to reference resources of use to activists and journalists, as well as a blog.

BIBLIOGRAPHY

"About the Library." Biblioteca Alexandrina. Accessed December 1, 2013. http://www.bibalex.org/aboutus/overview_en.aspx.

Afanasayev, V.G. *Dialectical Materialism*. New York: International Publishers, 1987.

Alabi, Jaena. "'Race is a Social Construct that Does Not Exist': What Librarians Have to Say about Racism in the Profession." Poster presented at the 2014 American Library Association Annual Conference, Las Vegas, NV, June 26-July 1, 2014.

Althusser, Louis. "Contradiction and Overdetermination: Notes for an Investigation." In *For Marx*, translated by Ben Brewster, 87-128. London: Penguin Press, 1965.

———. "Ideology and the Ideological State Apparatuses." In *Lenin and Philosophy and Other Essays*, translated by Ben Brewster, 86-126. New York: Monthly Review Press, 2001.

American Library Association. "Free Access to Libraries for Minors: An Interpretation of the Library Bill of Rights." In *Intellectual Freedom Manual*, 8th ed., 136-138. Chicago, IL: American Library Association, 2010.

———. "Library Bill of Rights," In *Intellectual Freedom Manual*, 8th ed., 49-61. Chicago, IL: American Library Association, 2010.

———. "Universal Right to Free Expression," In *Intellectual Freedom Manual*, 8th ed., 195-197. Chicago, IL: American Library Association, 2010.

Arendt, Hannah. *The Origins of Totalitarianism*. San Francisco, CA: Harcourt Brace, 1973.

Aronowitz, Stanley and Henry A. Giroux, *Education Still under Siege*. 2nd edition. Westport, CT: Bergin & Garvey, 1993.

Association of Research Libraries. *ARL Statistics, 2011-2012 Survey*. Edited by M Kyrillidou, S. Morris, and G. Roebuck. Washington, DC: Association of Research Libraries, 2013.

Bales, Stephen. "Occupy Elsevier." *Information for Social Change* 32 (Summer/Autumn 2012): 7-9. http://libr.org/isc/issues/ISC32/ISC32.pdf.

———. "Academic Library as Crypto-Temple." In *Class and Librarianship: Essays at the Intersection of Information*, edited by Erik Estep and Nathaniel Enright. Sacramento,CA: Library Juice Press, forthcoming.

Bales, Stephen and Lea Susan Engle. "The Counterhegemonic Academic Librarian: A Call to Action." *Progressive Librarian* 40 (2012): 16-40.

Ball, Stephen J. "Performativity, Commodification and Commitment: An I-Spy Guide to the Neoliberal University." *British Journal of Educational Studies* 60, no. 1 (2012): 17-28.

Balsamini, Luigi. "Libraries and Archives of the Anarchist Movement in Italy." *Progressive Librarian* 40 (Fall/Winter 2012), 1-15.

Battles, Mathew. *Library: An Unquiet History*. New York: W.W. Norton, 2003.

Berman, Sanford. *Prejudices and Antipathies: A Tract on the LC Subject Headings Concerning People*. Metuchen, NJ: Scarecrow Press, 1971.

Borges, Jorge Luis. "Poem of the Gifts." In *Dream Tigers*. Translated by Mildred Boyer and Harold Morland, 55-56. Austin, TX: University of Texas Press, 1965.

Bostick, Sharon. "The Development and Validation of the Library Anxiety Scale." PhD diss., Wayne State University, 1992.

Brand, Barbara Elizabeth. "Sex-Typing in Education for Librarianship: 1870-1920." In *The Status of Women in Librarianship: Historical, Sociological, and Economic Issues*, edited by Kathleen M. Heim, 29-49. New York: Neal-Schuman, 1983.

Budd, John M. "Toward a Practical and Normative Ethics for Librarianship." *Library Quarterly* 76, no. 3 (July 2006): 251-269.

———. *Self-Examination: The Present and Future of Librarianship*. Westport, CT: Libraries Unlimited, 2008.

Buick, Adam. "Joseph Dietzgen,"*Radical Philosophy* 10 (1975): 3-7.

Bukharin, Nikolai. *Historical Materialism: A System of Sociology*. Mansfield Centre, CT: Martino Publishing, 2013.

Burns, Tony. "Joseph Dietzgen and the History of Marxism." *Science & Society* 66, no. 2 (Summer, 2002): 202-227.

Buschman, John. "On Libraries and the Public Sphere." *Library Philosophy and Practice* 7, no. 2, (Spring, 2005). http://www.webpages.uidaho.edu/~mbolin/buschman.htm.

Buschman, John., Rosenzweig, Mark., and Elaine Harger. "The Clear Imperative for Involvement: Librarians Must Address Social Issues. " *American Libraries* 25, no. 6 (June 1994): 575-576.

Campbell, Joseph with Bill Moyers. *The Power of Myth*. New York: Doubleday, 1988).

Chalmers, David J. "Consciousness and Its Place in Nature." In *Blackwell Guide to the Philosophy of Mind*. Blackwell, edited by Stephen P. Stich and Ted A. Warfield, 102-142. Malden, MA: Blackwell, 2003.

Chartered Institute of Library and Information Professionals. "Ethical Principles for Library and Information Professionals." accessed August 6, 2014, http://www.cilip.org.uk/cilip/about/ethics/ethical-principles.

Coffman, Steve. "What if You Ran Your Library Like a Bookstore." *American Libraries* 29, no. 3 (March 1998), 40-46.

Cohen, G. A. *If You're an Egalitarian, How Come You're so Rich?* Cambridge, MA: Harvard University Press, 2000).

Collins, Nina. *The Library in Alexandria and the Bible in Greek.* Leiden: Brill, 2000.

Cowell, Penny. "Not All in the Mind: The Virile Profession," *Library Review* 29, no. 3 (1980), 167-175.

Cummins, J. *Language, Power and Pedagogy: Bilingual Children in the Crossfire.* Clevedon, England: Multilingual Matters, Ltd, 2000.

D'Angelo, Ed. *Barbarians at the Gates of the Public Library: How Postmodern Consumer Capitalism Threatens Democracy, Civil Education and the Public Good.* Duluth, MN: Library Juice Press, 2006.

Dana, John Cotton. *Libraries: Addresses and Essays.* White Plains, NY: H.W. Wilson Company, 1916.

Dick, Archie. "Library and Information Science as a Social Science: Neutral and Normative Conceptions." *Library Review* 65, no. 2 (1995): 216-235.

Dietzgen, Eugene."Joseph Dietzgen: A Sketch of His Life." In *Some of the Philosophical Essays on Socialism and Science, Religion, Ethics, Critique-of-Reason and the World-at-large,* by Joseph Dietzgen, edited by Eugene Dietzgen and Joseph Dietzgen, Jr., translated by M. Berr and Th. Rothstein, 7-33. Chicago: IL: Charles H. Kerr, 1917.

Dietzgen, Joseph. *The Positive Outcome of Philosophy: The Nature of Human Brain-Work, Letters on Logic, The Positive Outcome of Philosophy.* Translated by W.W. Craik. Chicago, IL: Charles H. Kerr & Company, 1906.

———. *Some of the Philosophical Essays on Socialism and Science, Religion, Ethics, Critique-of-Reason and the World-at-large.* Edited by Eugene Dietzgen and Joseph Dietzgen, Jr. Translated by M. Berr and Th. Rothstein. Chicago, IL: Charles H. Kerr, 1917.

———. *The Nature of Human Brainwork: An Introduction to Dialectics.* Oakland, PA: PM Press 2010.

Dix, T. Keith. "'Public Libraries' in Ancient Rome: Ideology and Reality," *Libraries and Culture* 29, no. 3 (1994): 282-296.

Doherty, John J., "Towards Self-Reflection in Librarianship: What is Praxis?" In *Questioning Library Neutrality: Essays from Progressive Librarian*, edited by Alison Lewis, 108-118. Duluth, MN: Library Juice Press, 2008.

Doughty, Howard A. "Steps to the Corporate Classroom: A Propositional Inventory." *College Quarterly* 11, no. 4 (2008). http://www.collegequarterly.ca/2008-vol11-num04-fall/doughty.html.

Eagleton, Terry. "Ideology and Its Vicissitudes." In *Mapping Ideology.* Edited by Slavoj Žižek, 179-226. London: Verso, 1994.

Ecklund, Elaine Howard and Chrisopher P. Scheitle. "Religion among Academic Scientists: Distinctions, Disciplines, and Demographics." *Social Problems* 54, no. 2 (May 2007): 289-307.

Eliade, Mircea. *The Sacred and the Profane: The Nature of Religion.* Translated by William A. Trask. New York: Harcourt Brace, 1987.

Engels, Friedrich. *Anti-Dühring: Herr Eugen Dühring's Revolution in Science.* Edited by C.P. Dutt. Translated by Emile Burns. New York: International Publishers, 1939.

———. *Dialectics of Nature*. Edited and translated by Clemens Dutt. New York: International Publishers, 1940.

———. *Feuerbach: The Roots of the Socialist Philosophy*. Translated by Austin Lewis. New York: Mondial, 2009.

Enright, Nathaniel. "The Violence of Information Literacy: Neoliberalism and the Human as Capital." In *Information Literacy and Social Justice: Radical Professional Practice*, edited by Lua Gregory and Shana Higgins, 16-38. Sacramento, CA: Library Juice Press, 2013.

Erskine, Andrew. "Culture and Power in Ptolemaic Egypt: The Museum and Library of Alexandria." *Greece & Rome*, 2nd Ser., 42, no. 1 (April 1995): 38-48.

Farmer, Brian R. *American Political Ideologies: An Introduction to the Major Systems of Thought in the 21st Century*. Jefferson, NC: McFarland & Company, 2006.

Feather, N.T. "Protestant Ethic, Conservatism, and Values." *Journal of Personality and Social Psychology* 46, no. 5 (1984): 1132-1141.

Feuerbach, Ludwig. *The Essence of Christianity*. Translated by George Eliot. New York: Harper & Brothers, 1957.

Freeden, Michael. *Ideology: A Very Short Introduction*. Oxford, UK: Oxford University Press, 2003.

Freire, Paulo, *Pedagogy of the Oppressed*. Translated by Myra Bergman Ramos. New York: Continuum, 1970.

Fukuyama, Francis. *The End of History and the Last Man*. New York: The Free Press, 1992.

Fung, Yu-Lan. "The Struggle between Materialism and Idealism in the History of Chinese Philosophy in Terms of Several Major Problems in Chinese Philosophy." *Chinese Studies in History and Philosophy: A Journal of Translations* 2, no. 4 (1969), 3-27.

Gadotti, Moacir. *Pedagogy of Praxis: A Dialectical Philosophy of Education.* Translated by John Milton. Albany, NY: State University of New York Press, 1996.

Gane, Nicholas. "Computerized Capitalism: The Media Theory of Jean-François Lyotard." *Information, Communication & Society* 6, no. 3 (2003): 435.

Gervasio, Darcy, Angela Ecklund, and Arieh Ross. "Library Research for the 99%: Reaching Out to the Occupy Wall Street Movement." *Urban Library Journal* 19, no. 1 (2013). http://ojs.gc.cuny.edu/index.php/urbanlibrary/article/view/1398/pdf_10.

Gollobin, Ira. *Dialectical Materialism: Its Laws, Categories, and Practice.* New York: Petras Press, 1986.

Gorman, Michael. *Our Enduring Values: Librarianship in the 21st Century.* Chicago, IL: American Library Association, 2000.

Gorter, Herman. "Historical Materialism." Marxists.org. Accessed January 2, 2014. https://www.marxists.org/archive/gorter/1920/historical-materialism.htm.

Gramsci, Antonio. *Selections from the Prison Notebooks.* Edited and translated by Quinton Hoare and Geoffrey Nowell Smith. New York: International Publishers, 1971.

Habermas, Jürgen. *Knowledge and Human Interests.* Translated by Jeremy J. Shapiro. Boston, MA: Beacon Press, 1971.

Harrington, Michael. *Socialism: Past and Future.* New York: Arcade Publishing, 1989.

Harris, Michael H. "The Role of the Public Library in American Life," *University of Illinois Graduate School of Library Science Occasional Papers* 117 (1972): 1-42.

———. *History of Libraries in the Western World.* Compact textbook ed. Metuchen, NJ: Scarecrow Press, 1984.

———. "State, Class, and Cultural Reproduction: Toward a Theory of Library Service in the United States." *Advances in Librarianship* 14 (1986): 211-252.

Heraclitus. *Fragments: The Collected Wisdom of Heraclitus.* Translated by Brooks Haxton. New York: Viking, 2001.

Hoepfner, Wolfram. *On Greek Libraries and Bookcases.* Berlin: de Gruyter, 1996.

Innis, Harold A. *The Bias of Communication.* Toronto: University of Toronto Press, 1951.

Jackson, H.J. *Marginalia: Readers Writing in Books.* New Haven, CT: Yale University Press, 2001.

James, William. *Essays in Radical Empiricism.* New York: Longmans, Green and Co., 1912.

Jenson, Robert. "The Myth of the Neutral Professional." In *Questioning Library Neutrality: Essays from Progressive Librarian*, edited by Alison Lewis, 89-96. Duluth, MN: Library Juice Press, 2008.

Jiao, Qun G. and Anthony J. Onwuegbuzie. "Perfectionism and Library Anxiety among Graduate Students." *Journal of Academic Librarianship* 25, no. 5 (1998): 365-371.

Kettler, David and Volker Meja. *Karl Mannheim and the Crisis of Liberalism: The Secret of These New Times.* New Brunswick, NJ: Transaction Publishers, 1995.

Knapp, John C., and David J. Siegel. *The Business of Higher Education.* 3rd ed. Santa Barbara, CA: Praeger, 2009.

Knapp, Patricia A. "The Library as a Complex Organization: Implications for Library Education." In *Towards a Theory of Librarianship: Papers in Honor of Jesse Hauk Shera*, edited by Conrad H. Rawski, 471-94. Metuchen, NJ: Scarecrow Press, 1973.

Knowlton, Charles. *Elements of Modern Materialism*. Adams, MA: A. Oakey, 1829.

Knowlton, Steven A. "Three Decades since Prejudices and Antipathies; A Study of Changes in the Library of Congress Subject Headings." *Cataloging & Classification Quarterly* 40, no. 2 (2005): 123-145.

Kramer, Samuel Noah. *History Begins at Sumer: Thirty-Nine Firsts in Man's Recorded History*. 3rd ed. Philadelphia: University of Pennsylvania Press, 1981.

Krapivin, Vassilii. *What is Dialectical Materialism?* Moscow: Progress Publishers, 1985.

Kuhn, Thomas S. *The Structure of Scientific Revolutions*. 3rd ed. Chicago, IL: University of Chicago Press, 1996.

Laakso, Mikael, Patrik Welling, Helena Bukvova, Linus Nyman, Bo-Christer Bjork, and Turid Hedlund. "The Development of Open Access Journal Publishing from 1993 to 2009." *PLoS ONE* 6, no. 6 (2011). http://journals.plos.org/plosone/article?id=10.1371/journal.pone.0020961.

Lao-Tse. *Dao De Jing*. Translated by Edmund Ryden. Oxford, UK: Oxford University Press, 2008.

Lenin, V.I. *What is to Be Done? Burning Questions of our Movement*. New York: International Publishers, 1969.

———. *Materialism and Empirio-Criticism: Critical Comments on a Reactionary Philosophy*. New York: International Publishers, 1972.

———. "Letter to Inessa Armand." In *Lenin Collected Works*, vol. 35. Translated by Andrew Rothstein. Moscow: Progress Publishers, 1976.

———. *Philosophical Notebooks, Collected Works*, vol. 38. Translated by Clemence Dutt. Edited by Stewart Smith. Moscow: Progress Publishers, 1976.

Leong, Nancy. "Racial Capitalism." *Harvard Law Review* 126, no. 8 (2013): 2151-2226.

Lévi-Strauss, Claude. "The Structural Study of Myth." *Journal of American Folklore* 68, no. 270 (1955): 428-444.

Lewis, Alison, ed. *Questioning Library Neutrality: Essays from Progressive Librarian*. Duluth, MN: Library Juice Press, 2008.

Lewis, David W. "From Stacks to the Web: The Transformation of Academic Library Collecting." *College and Research Libraries* 74, no. 2 (March 2013): 159-176.

Li, LiLi. *Emerging Technologies for Academic Libraries in the Digital Age*. Oxford, UK: Chandos Publishing, 2009.

Lowenthal, Helen. "A Healthy Anger." *Library Journal* 1 (1 September, 1971): 2597-99.

Lukacs, Gyorgy. *History and Class Consciousness: Studies in Marxist Dialectics*. Translated by Rodney Livingstone. London: Merlin Press, 1971.

Mannheim, Karl. *Ideology & Utopia: An Introduction to the Sociology of Knowledge*. San Diego, CA: Harcourt. 1936.

Marx, Karl. "Marx to Kugelmann in Hanover, 6 March 1868," Marxists.org. Accessed July 14, 2014. https://www.marxists.org/archive/marx/works/1868/letters/68_03_06-abs.htm.

———. *Capital: A Critique of the Political Economy*. Vol I. Translated by Ben Fowkes. London: Penguin Books, 1976.

———. "A Contribution to the Critique of Hegel's Philosophy of Right." In *Early Writings*, translated by Rodney Livingstone and Gregor Benton, 244-257. London: Penguin, 1992.

———. "Theses on Feuerbach." In *The German Ideology*, by Karl Marx and Friedrich Engels, 569-74. Amherst, NY: Prometheus Books, 1998.

———. *Wage-Labour and Capital.* New York: International Publishers, 1933.

Marx, Karl and Friedrich Engels. "Manifesto of the Communist Party." In *Economic and Philosophic Manuscripts of 1844*, translated by Martin Milligan, 203-243. Amherst, NY: Prometheus Books, 1988.

———. *The German Ideology.* Amherst, NY: Prometheus Books, 1998.

———. *Selected Correspondence 1846-1895: With Commentary and Notes*, The Marxist-Leninist Library, Vol. 9. London: Lawrence & Wishart, 1936.

Maxwell, Nancy Kalikow. *Sacred Stacks: The Higher Purpose of Libraries and Librarianship.* Chicago, IL: American Library Association, 2006.

McLellan, David. *Ideology.* Minneapolis, MN: University of Minnesota Press, 1986.

"Microaggressions in Librarianship." Microaggressions in Librarianship. Accessed November 15, 2014. http://lismicroaggressions.tumblr.com/archive.

Norton, Daniel, Mandy Henk, Betsy Fagin, Jaime Taylor, and Zachary Loeb. "Occupy Wall Street Librarians Speak Out." *Progressive Librarian* 38/39 41 (2013): 3-16.

O'Donnell, James J. *Avatars of the Word: From Papyrus to Cyberspace.* Cambridge, MA: Harvard University Press, 1998.

Ollman, Bertell. "Market Mystification in Capitalist and Market Socialist Societies." Dialectical Materialism: The Writings of Bertell Ollman. Accessed November 15, 2015. http://www.nyu.edu/projects/ollman/docs/market_mystification.php.

———. *Alienation: Marx's Conception of Man in Capitalist Society.* Cambridge, UK: Cambridge University Press, 1971.

———. *Dance of the Dialectic: Steps in Marx's Method.* Urbana, IL: University of Illinois Press, 2003.

Oppenheim, A. Leo. "Assyriology—Why and How? *Current Anthropology* 1, nos. 5-6 (1960): 36-39.

———. *Ancient Mesopotamia: Portrait of a Dead Civilization*. Rev. ed. Chicago, IL: University of Chicago Press, 1964.

Orozco, Cynthia Mari, Elvia Arroyo-Ramirez, Rose L. Chou, and Anni Pho. "Increasing the Diversity Dialogue: Sharing Our Experiences with Microagressions in Librarianship." Poster presented at the 2014 American Library Association Annual Conference, Las Vegas, NV, June 26-July 1, 2014.

Pannekoek, Anton. *Anthropogenesis: A Study of the Origin of Man*. Amsterdam: North-Holland Publishing Company, 1953.

———. *Lenin as Philosopher: A Critical Examination of Philosophical Basis of Leninism*. Rev. ed. Edited by Lance Byron Richey. Milwaukee, WI: Marquette University Press, 2003.

Pettigrew, Karen and Lynne E.F. McKechnie. "The Use of Theory in Information Science Research." *Journal of the American Society for Information Science and Technology* 52, no. 1 (2001): 62-73.

Powell, Ronald R. "Competence for Ph.D. Students in Library and Information Science." *Journal of Education for Library and Information Science* 36, no. 4 (Fall 1995): 319-29.

Raber, Douglas. "Librarians as Organic Intellectuals: A Gramscian Approach to Blind Spots and Tunnel Vision." *Library Quarterly* 68, no. 1 (2003): 33-53.

———. "Hegemony, Historic Blocs, and Capitalism: Antonio Gramsci in Library and Information Science," In *Critical Theory for Library and Information Science: Exploring the Social from Across the Disciplines*, edited by Gloria J. Leckie, Lisa M. Given, and John Buschman, 143-160. Santa Barbara, CA: Libraries Unlimited, 2010.

Reichmann, Felix. *The Sources of Western Literacy: The Middle Eastern Civilizations*. Westport, CT: Greenwood Press, 1980.

Richardson, Ernest Cushing, *Some Old Egyptian Librarians*. Berkeley, CA: Peacock Press, 1964.

Roberts, Peter. "Neoliberalism, Performativity and Research." *Review of Education* 53, no. 4 (2007): 349-365.

Rochelle, Carlton. "The Knowledge Business: Economic Issues of Access to Bibliographic Information." *College & Research Libraries* 46, no. 1 (1985): 5-12.

Rosenzweig, Mark. "Politics and Anti-Politics in Librarianship." In *Questioning Library Neutrality: Essays from Progressive Librarian*, edited by Alison Lewis, 5-7. Duluth, MN: Library Juice Press, 2008.

Rubin, Richard E. *Foundations of Library and Information Science*. New York: Neal-Schuman, 2000.

Sagan, Carl. *Cosmos*. 1st ed. New York: Random House, 1980.

Samek, Toni. *Intellectual Freedom and Social Responsibility in American Librarianship, 1967-1974*. Jefferson, NC: McFarland & Company, 2001.

Sayer, Derek, *The Violence of Abstraction: The Analytic Foundations of Historical Materialism*. Oxford, UK: Basil Blackwell, 1987.

Schmandt-Besserat, Denise. "The Earliest Precursor of Writing." *Scientific American* 238, no. 6 (June 1977): 50-58.

Screpanti, Ernesto. "Capitalist Forms and the Essence of Capitalism." *Review of International Political Economy* 6, no. 1 (1999): 1-26.

Scruton, Roger. "Scientism in the Arts and Humanities." *The New Atlantis* 40 (Fall 2013): 33-46.

Slaughter, Sheila, and Gary Rhoades. *Academic Capitalism and the New Economy: Markets, State, and Higher Education*. Baltimore, MA: John Hopkins University Press, 2004.

Sparanese, Ann. "Activist Librarianship: Heritage or Heresy? One Librarian's Two-Part List of Relevant and Thoughtful Reading for the Engaged Librarian and Involved Citizen." In *Questioning Library Neutrality: Essays from Progressive* Librarian, edited by Alison Lewis, 83-88. Duluth, MN: Library Juice, 2008;

Spinoza, Benedict. *Ethics*. Translated by W.H. White. Revised by A.H. Stirling. Ware, UK: Wordsworth Editions, 2001.

Stabile, Donald R. *Economics, Competition, and Academia: An Intellectual History of Sophism versus Virtue*. Cheltanham, UK: Edward Elgar, 2007.

Staikos, Konstantinos Sp. *The History of the Library in Western Civilization*, vol. 1: *From Minos to Cleopatra*. Translated by Timothy Cullen. New Castle, DE: Oak Knoll Press, 2004.

Sue, Derald Wing. *Microagressions in Everyday Life: Race, Gender, and Sexual Orientation*. Hoboken, NJ: Wiley, 2010.

Tegmark, Max. *Our Mathematical Universe: My Quest for the Ultimate Nature of Reality*. New York: Alfred A. Knopf, 2014.

Tierney, William G. *Building the Responsive Campus: Creating High Performance Colleges and Universities*. Thousand Oaks, CA: Sage, 1999.

Untermann, Ernest. *Science and Revolution*. Chicago, IL: Kerr, 1910.

Weber, Max. *The Protestant Ethic and the "Spirit" of Capitalism and Other Writings*. Edited and translated by Peter Baehr and Gordon C. Wells. New York: Penguin Books, 2002.

Wente, Edward F. "The Scribes of Ancient Egypt." In *Civilizations of the Ancient Near East*, 4 vols., edited by Jack M. Sasson, John Baines, Gary Beckman, and Karen S. Rubinson, 2211-2221. New York: Charles Scribner's Sons, 1995.

Wiegand, Wayne A. "Tunnel Visions and Blind Spots: What the Past Tells Us about the Present: Reflections on the Twentieth-Century History of American Librarianship. *Library Quarterly* 69, no. 1 (1999): 1-32.

Wisner, William H. *Whither the Postmodern Library? Libraries, Technology, and Education in the Information Age.* Jefferson, NC: McFarland & Company, 1999.

Wolff, Richard D. *Capitalism Hits the Fan: The Global Economic Meltdown and What to do about It.* Updated ed. Northampton, MA: Olive Branch Press, 2013.

Wright, Erik Olin. *Classes.* London: Verso, 1985.

Žižek, Slavoj. *The Parallax View.* Cambridge, MA: MIT Press, 2006.

———. *First as Tragedy, Then as Farce.* London: Verso, 2009.

Zwieg, Stefan. *Beware of Pity.* Translated by Phyllis and Trevor Blewitt. New York: New York Review Books, 2006.

About the Author

Stephen Bales is a Humanities and Social Sciences Librarian at Texas A&M University Libraries.

INDEX

A

academic libraries. *See also* **modern capitalist academic library**
  as historically hegemonic institutions, 102-11
  dynamic nature of, 2-5
Althusser, Louis
  For Marx, 162
American Library Association (ALA)
  counter-hegemony and, 128
  Library Bill of Rights, 79, 82-83
Association of College and Research Libraries (ACRL), 14n27

B

business model. *See* **corporatization**

C

Capital **(Marx), 159**
capitalism
  advanced. *See* neoliberalism
  library as apparatus for, 14-15
  Marx and Engels' critique of, 6
  neoliberal. *See* neoliberalism
  power relationships of, 30
  repercussions of modern, 7
central values of librarianship, 29-32
class society
  idealism and, 24
colleges and universities
  neoliberal transformation of, 10-12

Communist Manifesto **(Engels, Marx), 7, 62**
conscientização, 137-38, 166
corporatization of higher education
  academic libraries and, 6-10
  evolution of librarianship, 16
  idealist concern over, 12-13
  LIS pushback, 11-13, 14n27
critical thinking
  resources for LIS on, 160-62

D

democracy, 30-32
dialectics. *See also* **materialism**
  dialectical materialism, 25, 48-51, 152
  dialectical materialist monism, 138-40
  history of, 57-64
  principle of constant transformtion, 43, 74, 93-96
digital dark age, 126, 146
digital divide, 126, 151-52, 164
diversity, 32-34, 36

E

Engels, Friedrich
  Communist Manifesto, 7, 62
  German Ideology, The, 94, 96-97, 164
  Socialism: Utopian and Scientific, 158
evolution of librarianship, 16

F

Freire, Paulo, 119, 130
    conscientização, 137-38, 166
    oppression and, 136-38
    Pedagogy of the Oppressed, 166

G

German Ideology, The **(Engels, Marx), 94, 96-97, 164**

I

idealism. *See also* **materialism**
    non-dialectical objective, 24-27
        vs. dialectical materialism, 48
    objective, 24-29, 34
    theoretical vs. practical, 24
ideology
    problem of, 96-102
    resources for consciousness of, 162-65
Ideology & Utopia **(Mannheim), 164**
information technologies
    theory of commodification and, 10
Information for Social Change (UK group), 169

L

Lenin, V.I.,
    Materialism and Empirio-Criticism, 159
Leninism. *See also* **Marxism**
    dialectics and, 62-64, 72, 75

librarianship
    eight central values of, 29-30
libraries
    dynamic nature of, 2-5
Library Bill of Rights **(ALA), 79, 82-83**

M

Mannheim, Karl
    Ideology & Utopia, 164
Marx, Karl
    Capital, 159
    Communist Manifesto (Engels, Marx), 7, 62
    German Ideology, The, 94, 96-97, 164
Marxism. *See also* **Leninism**
    academic, 135
    critical analysis for hegemonic structures, 130-31
    dialectic material monism and, 60-68, 72, 82-84
    ideology and MCALs, 114-18
    libraries and, 4-7, 16, 37-38, 47-48, 104
Marxists Internet Archive, 169
materialism. *See also* **idealism.** *See also* **dialectics**
    dialectical, 25-26, 48-51, 152
        as social critique, 64-74
    communism and, 55
    non-dialectical objective idealism vs., 48
    history of, 57-64
    Lenin and, 73n36

MCALs and non-dialectical, 43-48
non-dialectical, 39-43
Materialism and Empirio-Criticism (Lenin), 159
Microagressions in Librarianship, 170
modern capitalist academic library (MCAL). *See also* **academic libraries**
  as sociocultural conservator, 119-20
  contradictory nature of, 74-83, 151
  counter-hegemony and, 120-24, 131-38
  online resources, 169-70
  ideology and, 111-20
  physical reality of, 51-53, 149-52
  resources for MCAL as terrain of struggle, 165-69
  systems of relations and, 83-92
  Truths of non-dialectical objective idealism and, 27-39

N
neo-capitalism. *See* **neoliberalism**
neoliberalism
  defined, 6
  education and, 11-14
  internal contradictions of, 7-9
  transformation of colleges and universities towards, 10
  values of, 8

non-dialectical objective idealism. *See under* **idealism**

O
Open Access movement, 144-45

P
Pedagogy of the Oppressed (Freire), 166
Progressive Librarians Guild, 170

Q
Quantity and quality
  economic success and, 9
  human social relations and, 141-44
  library services and, 144-47

R
Radical Librarians Collective, 170
Radical Reference, 170
Ranganathan, S.R.
  Five Laws of Librarianship, 34-36
reality
  as a web of codetermining relations, 10
  dialectics of total, 91-92
  three ways to view libraries in total, 23

S
social change, 125-27, 152-53
  counter-hegemonic librarianship, 131-38

LIS practitioners and, 127-31
Socialism (Engels), 158
Stalinism, 56, 63
Soviet Union
    dialectical material monism in, 56, 63-64

T

theoretical consciousness
    resources for expanding, 158-60
Truth, 26-27
    Democracy as, 30-32
    dialectical material monism and, 63, 70-71
    MCAL and, 27
    non-dialectical materialism and, 42-43
    non-dialectical objective idealism, 27, 30, 36

www.ingramcontent.com/pod-product-compliance
Lightning Source LLC
Chambersburg PA
CBHW021949290426
44108CB00012B/1002